Jon Shain

Gettin' Handy with the Blues

A Tribute to the Legacy of W.C. Handy

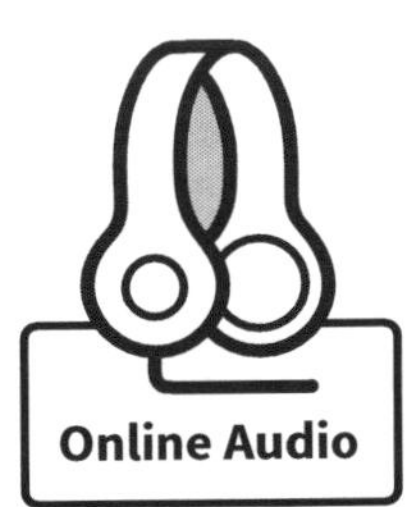

To access the online audio recording go to:
WWW.MELBAY.COM/31108MEB

Front cover design from CD artwork by FJ Ventre.
Back cover portrait photo of author by Jeff Fasano.

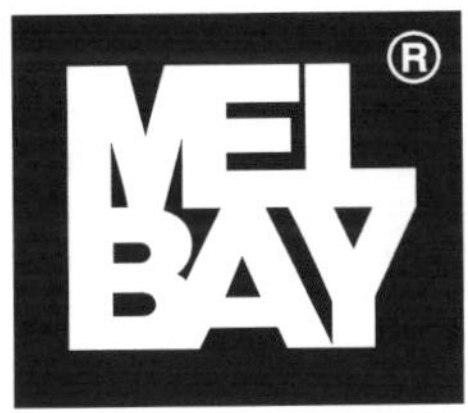

EXCLUSIVE SALES AGENT: MEL BAY PUBLICATIONS, INC.
WWW.MELBAY.COM

Contents

Foreword

In the spring of 2017, I was asked by Steve Kelly and the Craven Arts Council of New Bern, NC to tackle an interesting musical project. Steve was presenting a monthly concert series focusing on the music of the great 20th century American songwriters (think Gershwin, Porter, Cahn, etc.) and he asked me if I would do a show of all tunes by W. C. Handy, the "Father of the Blues". I distinctly remember replying, "But, Steve, that wasn't guitar music…" Steve told me, " That's exactly why I want you to do it". I knew it would be a huge undertaking, but I said yes – mainly due to Steve's unflagging enthusiasm for the project and his years of gracious hospitality to us traveling musicians.

I began to go through the original sheet music (where it was available), the original recordings on 78 rpm records (many of these can now be found as YouTube videos of people spinning records on Victrolas!), and later famous renditions of the material (such as the classic jazz album *Louis Armstrong plays W. C. Handy*). I quickly realized that I would have to re-key the compositions for my vocal (as many of the tunes were originally sung by women) and to figure out the best positions for playing on the guitar, allowing the melody to be picked alongside the rollicking and creative ragtime bass lines. I also had to alter a few of the lyrics to make the vernacular more easily understood and (more culturally acceptable to a modern listener), as well as changing the gender of the narrator sometimes.

In October of 2017, I premiered my new guitar and vocal arrangements with a concert in New Bern, presenting 16 tunes written by Handy and his related collaborators, along with historical background on all the selections. A week later, I went into Good Luck Studio in Chapel Hill, NC with my longtime musical partner FJ Ventre producing, and we tracked my favorite ten songs over the course of two days. The resulting album, *Getting Handy with the Blues - A Tribute to the Legacy of W. C. Handy* garnered some of the best reviews of my career, cracked the top 15 on Sirius XM's Bluesville chart, and elicited high praise from one of my fingerpicking heroes, Roy Book Binder who wrote me, "Jon, I figured it would be good... but I love what you've done with these old gems! A very worthy project... great arrangements, singing and pickin'...A totally original concept... Who knows where it will carry you…"

It's my great privilege to help in keeping this music alive. I hope you enjoy playing these tunes as much as I do!

Jon Shain, Durham, NC 2022

About the Tab Arrangements

As a largely improvisational blues player, my versions of these great compositions change from performance to performance. While the TAB's I've created do correspond with the versions found on my CD, *Gettin' Handy with the Blues - A Tribute to the Legacy of W. C. Handy*, they do not contain every verse of every song. Instead, I concentrated on bringing the vocal melody into the guitar parts, and on sharing some of my favorite single note riffs, bass ideas, and chord voicings. The CD can be used very well as a good reference for arrangement and feel, but the TAB's are not exact note-for-note transcriptions of what I played those two days in the studio.

The TAB notation includes hammer-ons, pull-offs, slides, bends, and rakes across strings. Pay special attention to the melody notes in the treble that often last longer than the bass notes. The chord diagrams at the top of the page are meant as a guide to the fingerings that will allow the passages to be played with most ease and fluidity. "N.C." means "no chord", denoting a passage that is largely melodic and easier played when not holding a chord in place.

This would be very hard music to play without playing fingerstyle. Alternating-thumb style (Piedmont picking or Travis-style) does largely rule the day in these guitar arrangements, as it captures the ragtime feel of the original piano arrangements. So a good "rule of thumb", if you will, is to look at the quarter notes in the bass as being picked with the right-hand thumb, and pick the melody notes with one or two fingers. That being said, one of the joys of ragtime guitar arrangements is the melodic movement in the bass, so many of the bass lines switch from simple alternating-thumb bass to lines that have the thumb staying on one string for several notes or even going to an eighth-note pattern at times.

About the Lyrics

The lyrics to Handy's songs (and many blues tunes, in general) have been subject to editing, personalization, and re-interpretation by many performers for a hundred years now. For the lyrics I have printed in this book, I went back to the original sets of lyrics and did my own editing, in some cases simplifying lines to fit with complicated guitar patterns. I also changed some lyrics to fit a male narrator and updated them sometimes when I felt the language originally used would be culturally inappropriate for today. The lyrics printed in this book are those that I sang on my CD of these tunes. While the TAB's don't have every verse transcribed, the lyrics printed here are grouped in the sections (A, B, C, etc) as they appear in the song.

About W. C. Handy

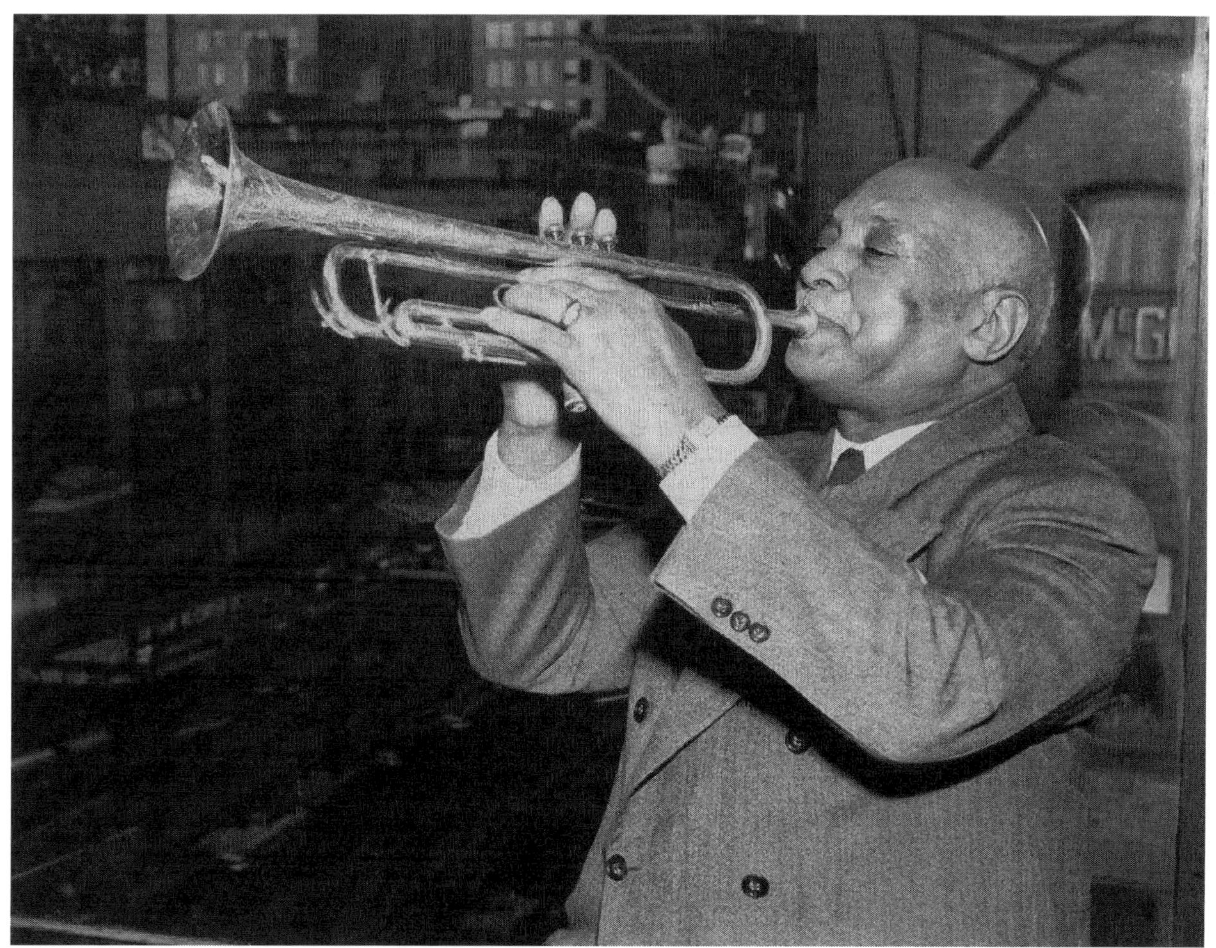

W. C. Handy

William Christopher Handy (1873 - 1958) was born in Florence, AL. A classically trained musician and composer, Handy delved into his people's blues music and became one of its greatest popularizers. He is known not only for his famous compositions, but for breaking color barriers in business with his own music publishing and recording companies. If you would like more information on the music or life of W. C. Handy, a great place to start is with his autobiography, *Father of the Blues*, originally published in 1941.

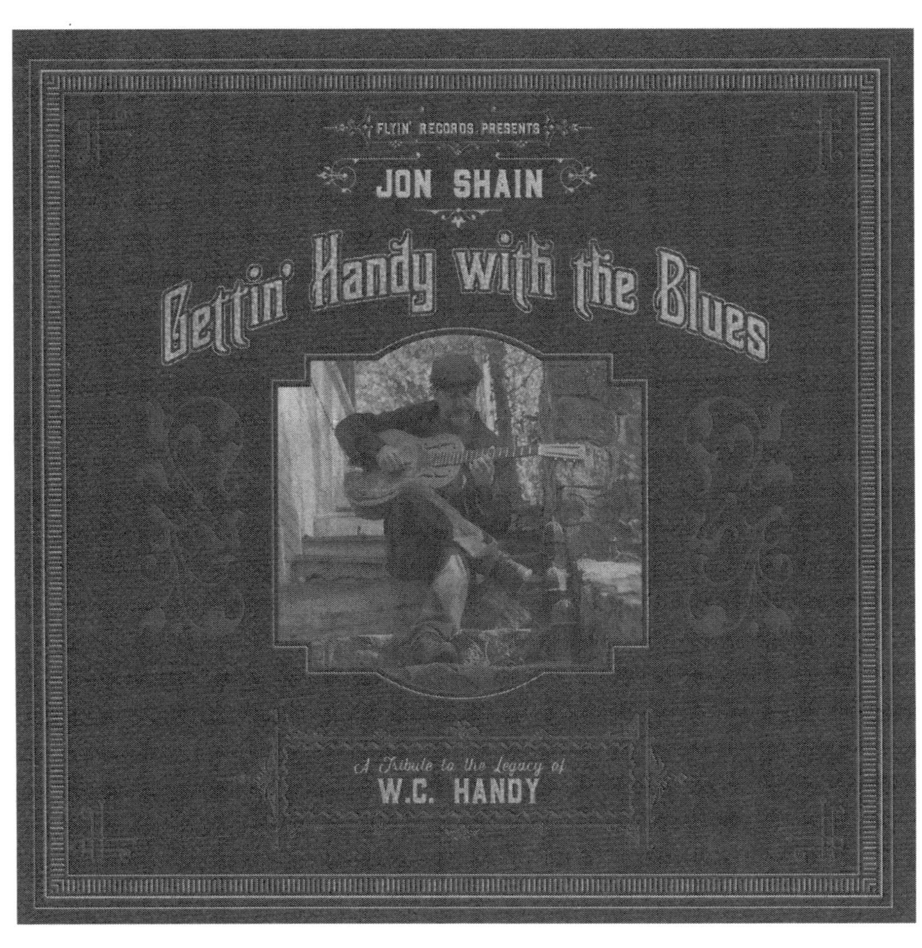
FLYIN' RECORDS PRESENTS
JON SHAIN
Gettin' Handy with the Blues
A Tribute to the Legacy of
W.C. HANDY

St. Louis Blues

Written by W. C. Handy

"St. Louis Blues" was published in 1914 by Pace and Handy in Memphis, TN, but the song was slow to gain popularity. Its first known performance was in 1914 by Charles Anderson, a popular female impersonator in Vaudeville. Ethel Waters learned the song from Anderson and began performing it in 1917. The song was first recorded by white Vaudeville singer Al Bernard in 1919, but it was Bessie Smith's 1925 recording on Columbia Records of "St. Louis Blues" that firmly established the song in the Great American Songbook.

A

I hate to see that evenin' sun go down
I hate to see that evenin' sun go down
'Cause my baby, she done left this town

If I feel tomorrow like I feel today
If I feel tomorrow like I feel today
I'll pack my trunk and make my getaway

B

St. Louis Woman, with her diamond rings
She pulls men around by her apron strings
If it weren't for powder and for store-bought hair
All the men around wouldn't go nowhere, nowhere

A

Got the St. Louis Blues, just as blue as I can be
That gal got a heart like a rock cast in the sea
Or else she wouldn't have gone so far from me

I love that girl like a schoolboy love his pie
I love that girl like a schoolboy love his pie
I love my baby till the day I die

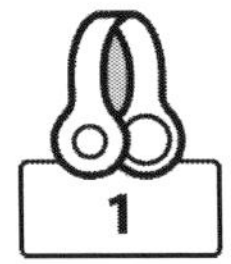

St. Louis Blues

by W. C. Handy (arranged for guitar by Jon Shain)

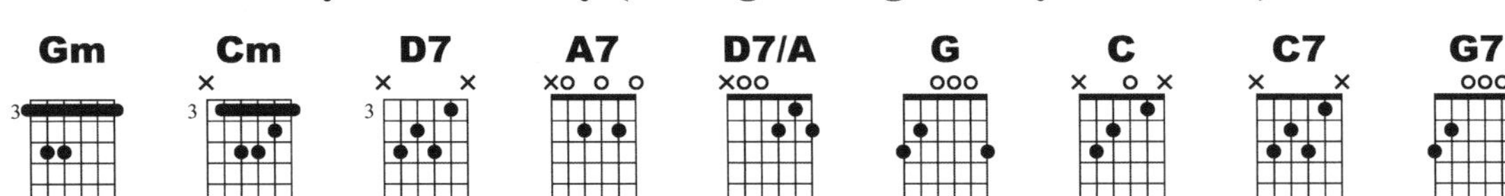

Standard tuning

♩ = 117

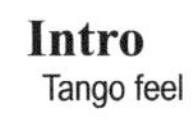

Intro
Tango feel

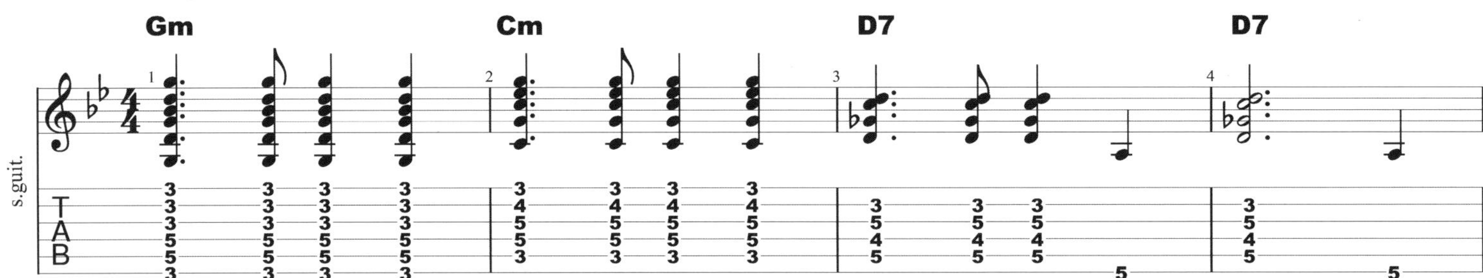

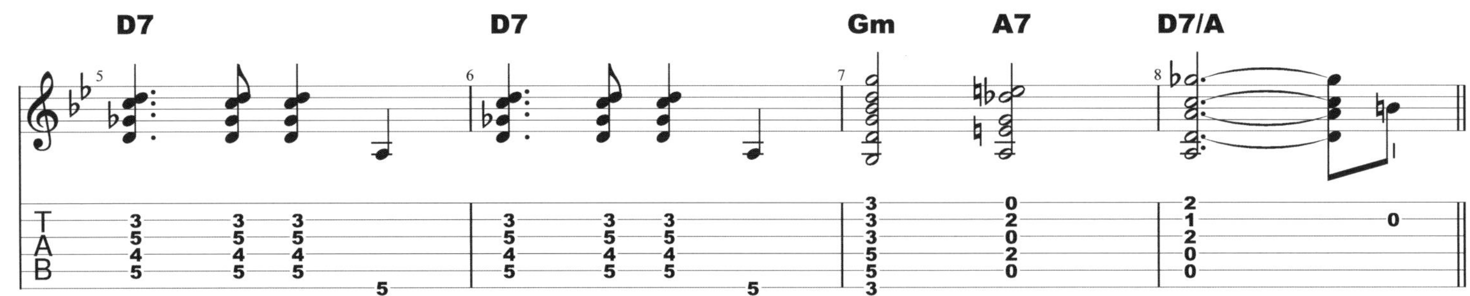

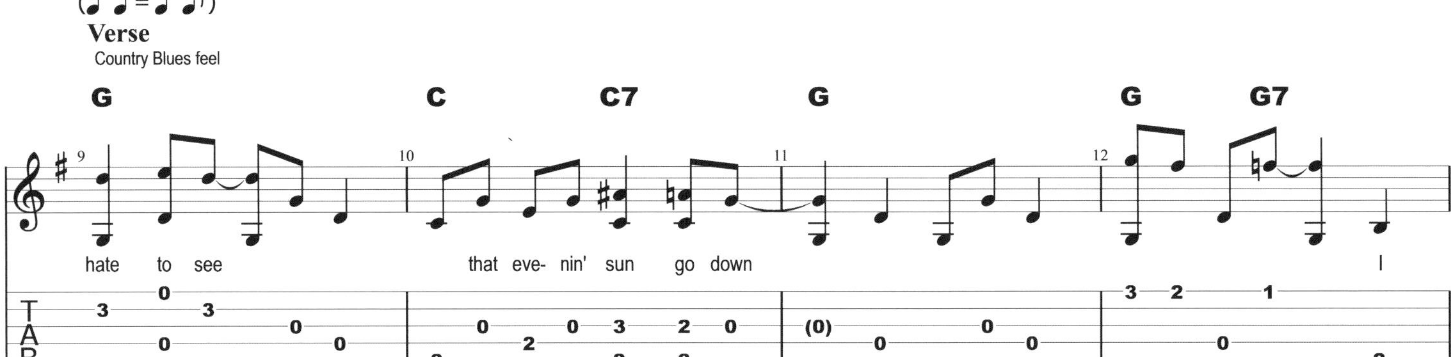

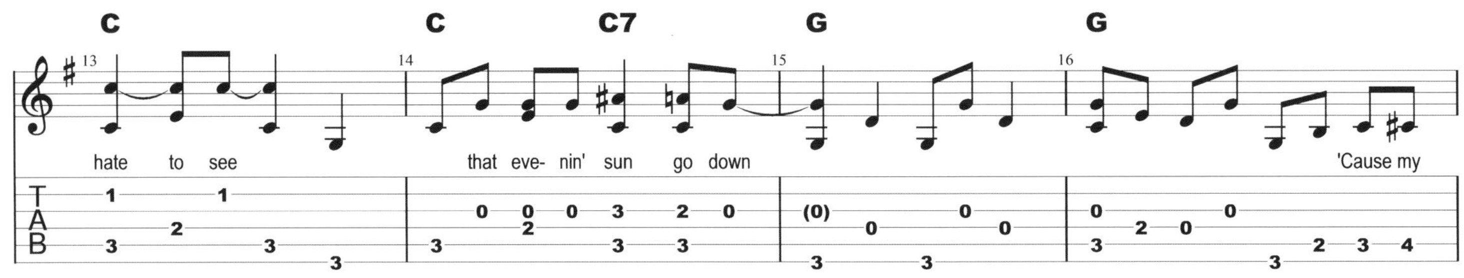

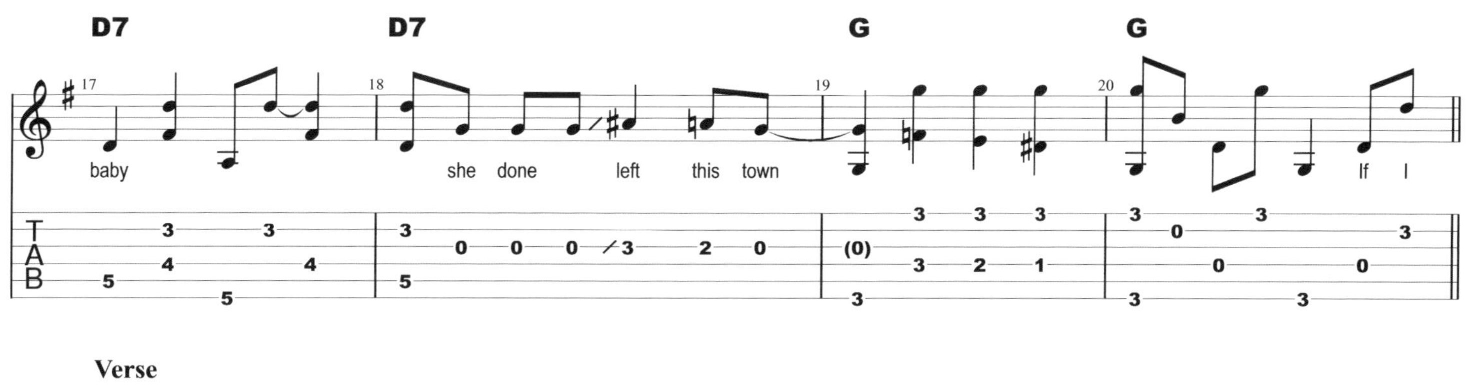
D7 D7 G G
baby she done left this town If I

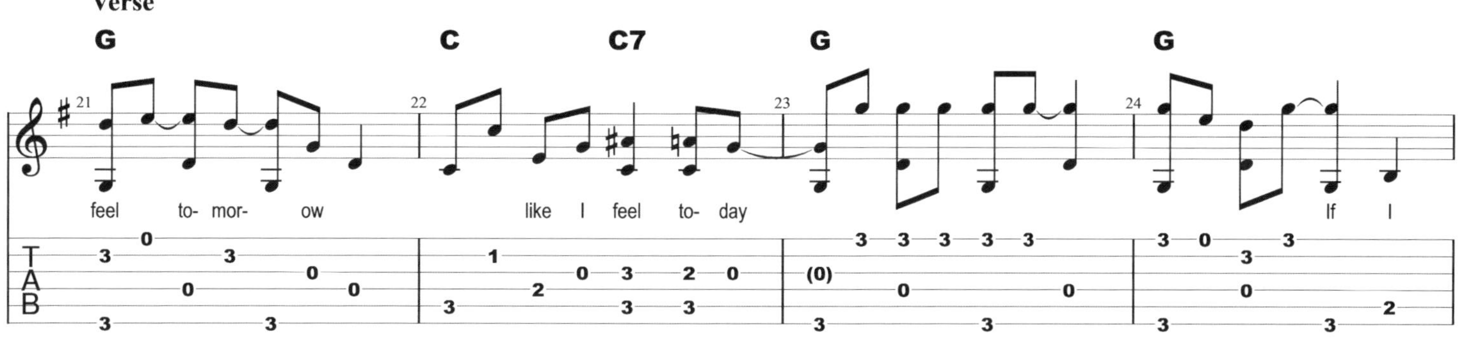
Verse
G C C7 G G
feel to- mor- ow like I feel to- day If I

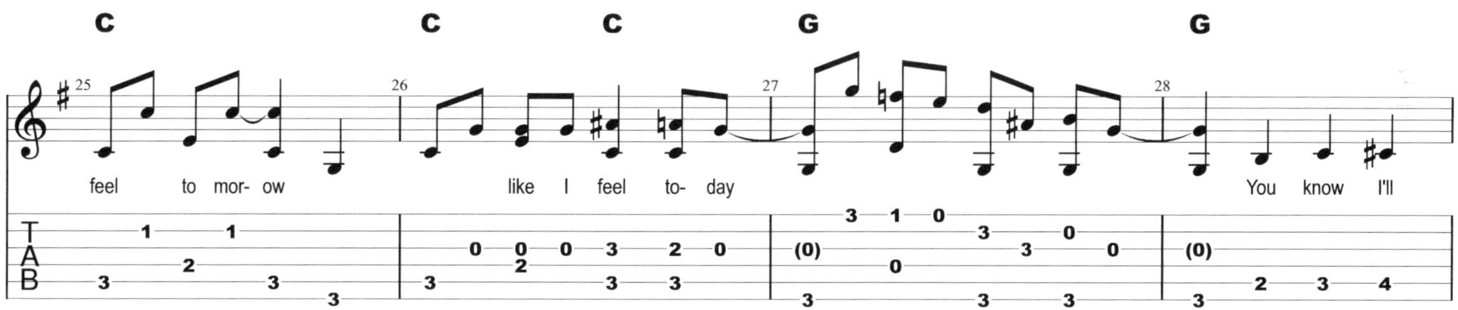
C C C G G
feel to mor- ow like I feel to- day You know I'll

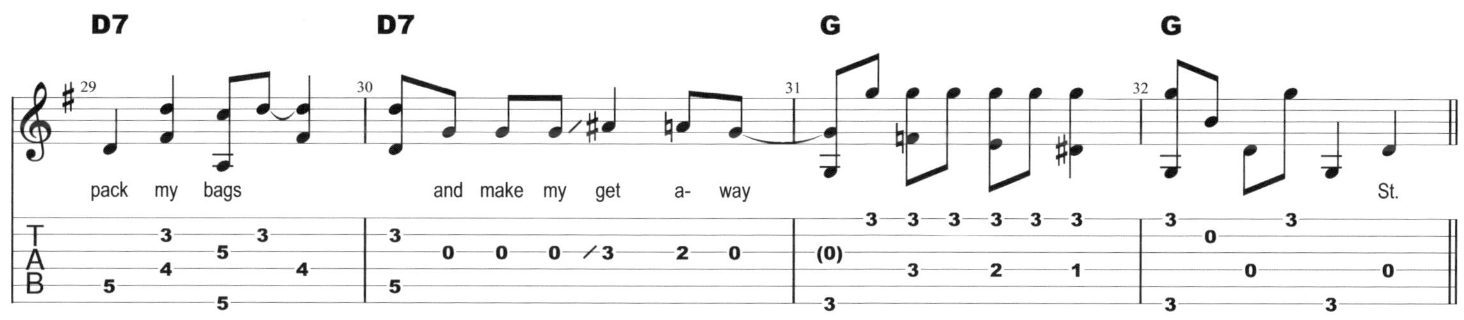
D7 D7 G G
pack my bags and make my get a- way St.

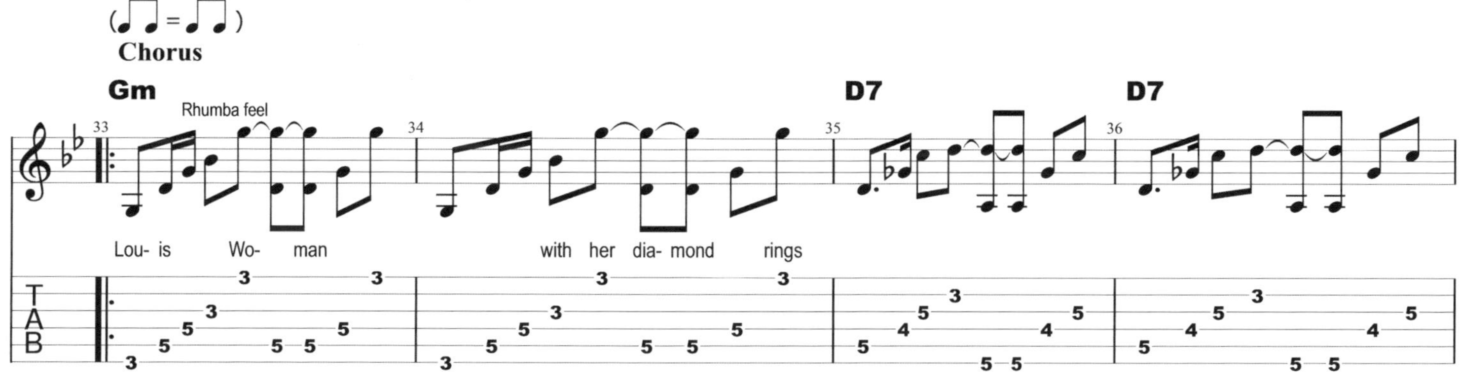
Chorus
Gm D7 D7
Rhumba feel
Lou- is Wo- man with her dia- mond rings

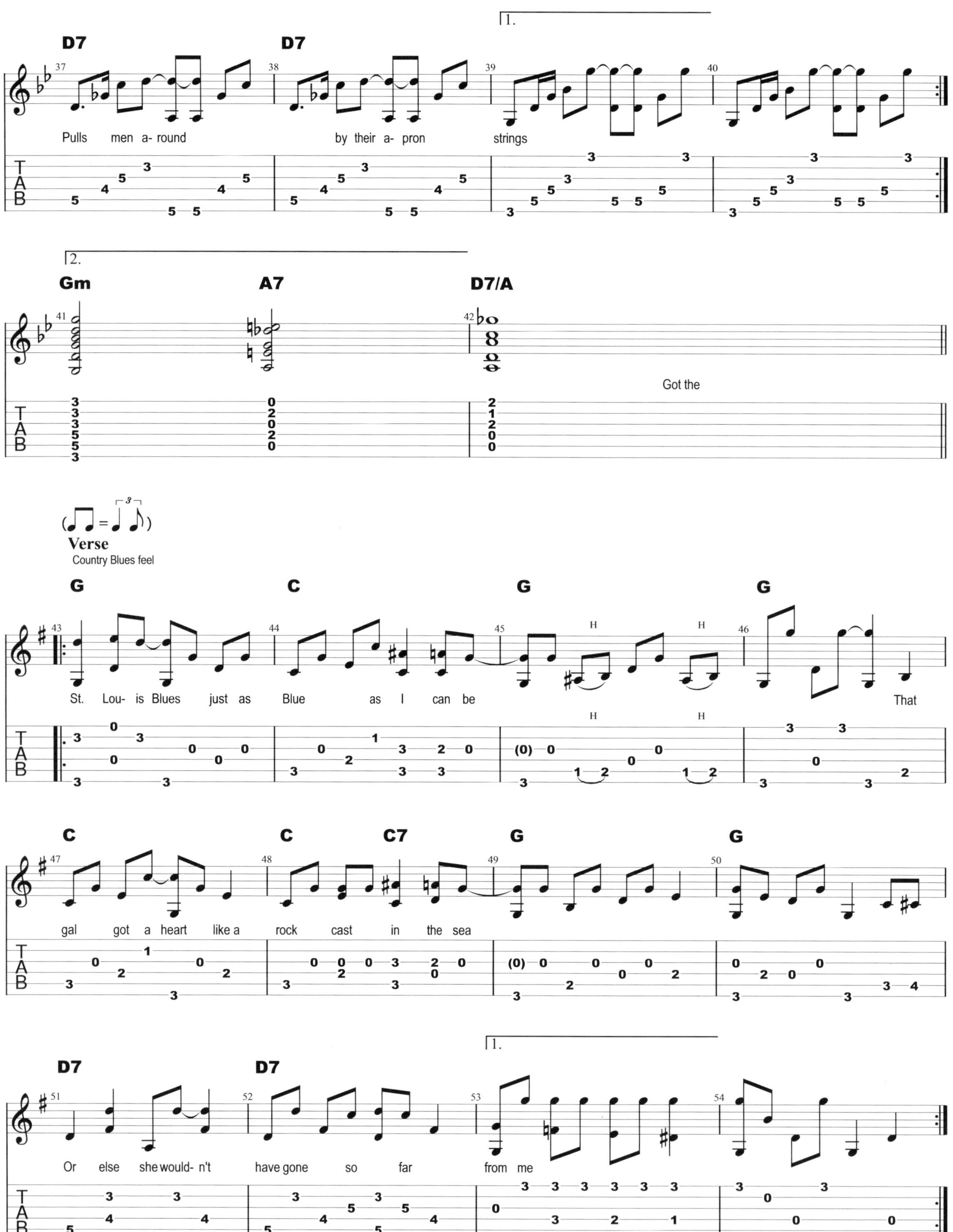
D7
D7
1.
Pulls men a- round
by their a- pron
strings
2.
Gm
A7
D7/A
Got the
Verse
Country Blues feel
G
C
G
G
St. Lou- is Blues just as Blue as I can be
That
C
C
C7
G
G
gal got a heart like a rock cast in the sea
D7
D7
1.
Or else she would- n't have gone so far from me

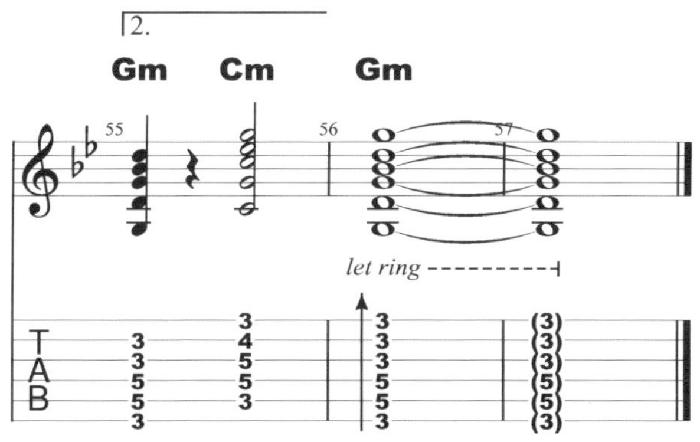

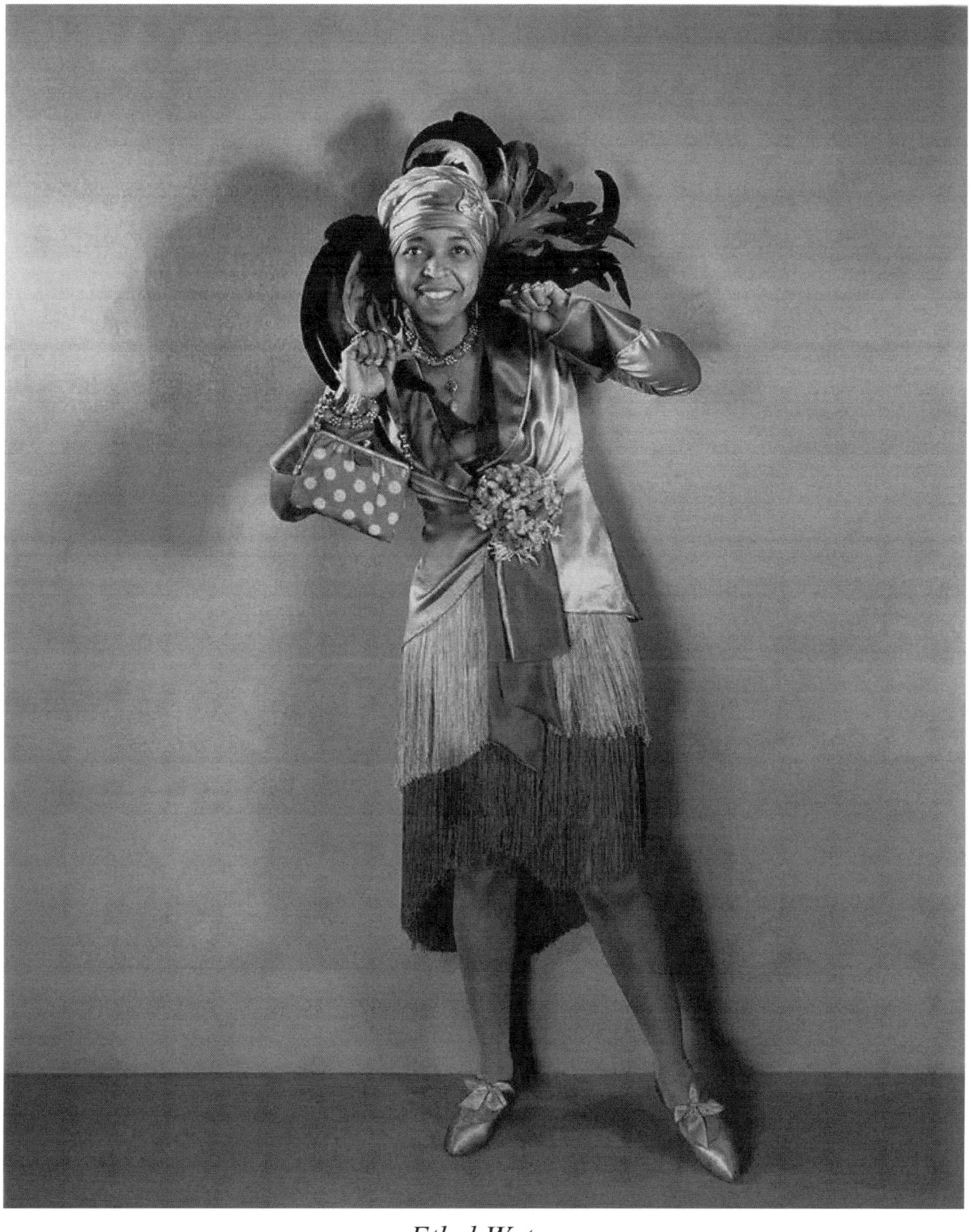

Ethel Waters

Memphis Blues

Written by W. C. Handy and George Norton

"The Memphis Blues" was first written as a campaign song for (or against) mayor E. H. Crump, who ended up being a boss in local politics for many years. Handy adapted the song to piano music and published it in 1911, making "The Memphis Blues" the first blues song to ever be published! The key changes in this song mark it as a composition outside of the more traditional folk blues forms, and may have made it more salable as a piece of music to be learned on the piano. Sometimes, I accidentally confuse the old politician's name with a modern one's when I'm performing this one. Wink, wink.

A

You want to be my gal, you to gotta give me forty dollars down
You want to be my gal, you to gotta give me forty dollars down
If you don't be my gal, your baby's gonna shake this town

B

Mister Crump don't allow no easy riders here
Mister Crump don't allow no easy riders here
We don't care what Mister Crump don't allow
We gonna barrelhouse anyhow
Mister Crump don't allow no easy riders here

If Mister Crump don't allow it, ain't gonna have it here
If Mister Crump don't allow it, ain't gonna have it here
We don't care what Mister Crump don't allow
We gonna barrelhouse anyhow
Mister Crump can go and catch his self some air

C

I'm goin' down the river, gonna take my rockin' chair
I'm goin' down the river, gonna take my rockin' chair
Blues over take me, I'm gonna rock from here

Oh, the Mississippi River, Mississippi River so wide
Mississippi River's so deep and wide
And the gal I love, she on the other side

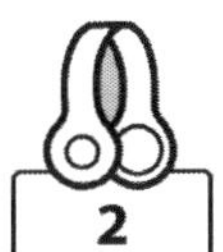

Memphis Blues

by W. C. Handy (arranged for guitar by Jon Shain)

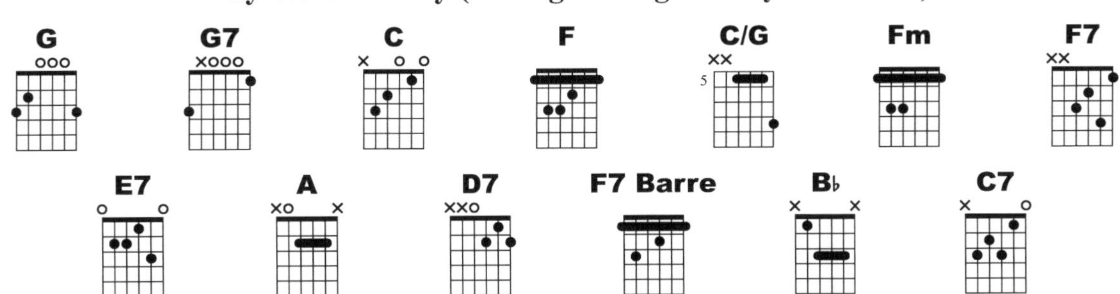

Standard tuning

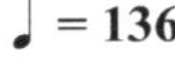

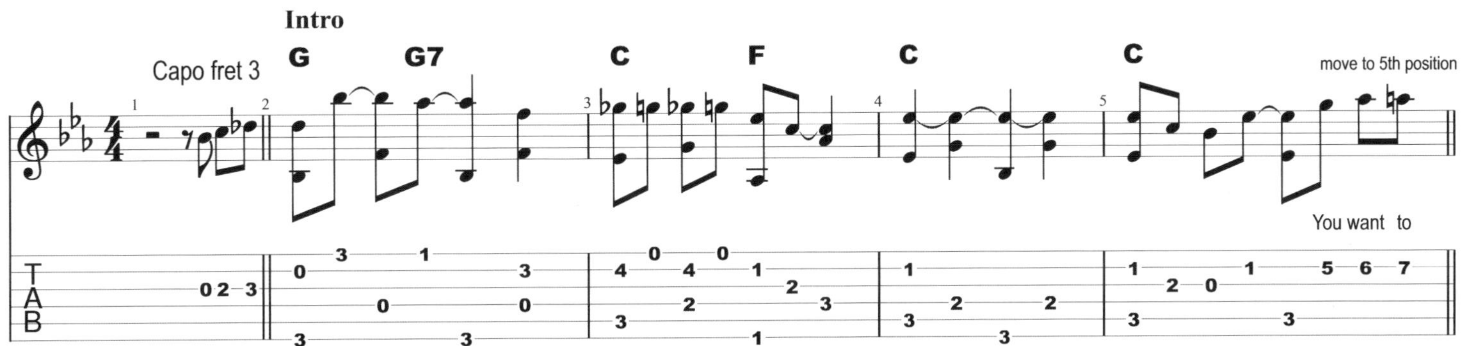

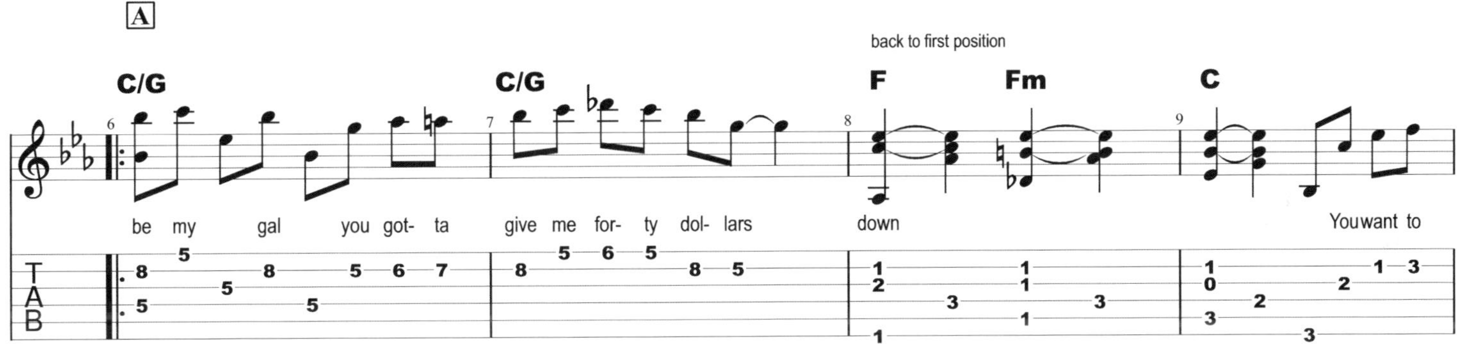

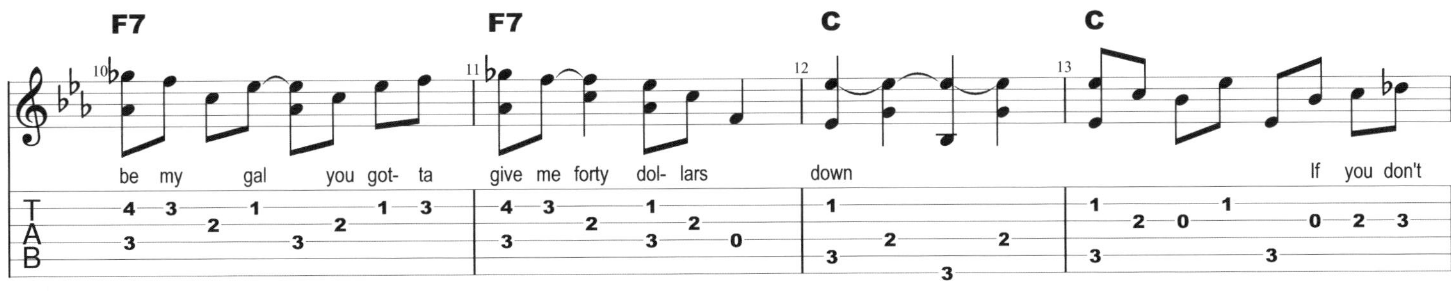

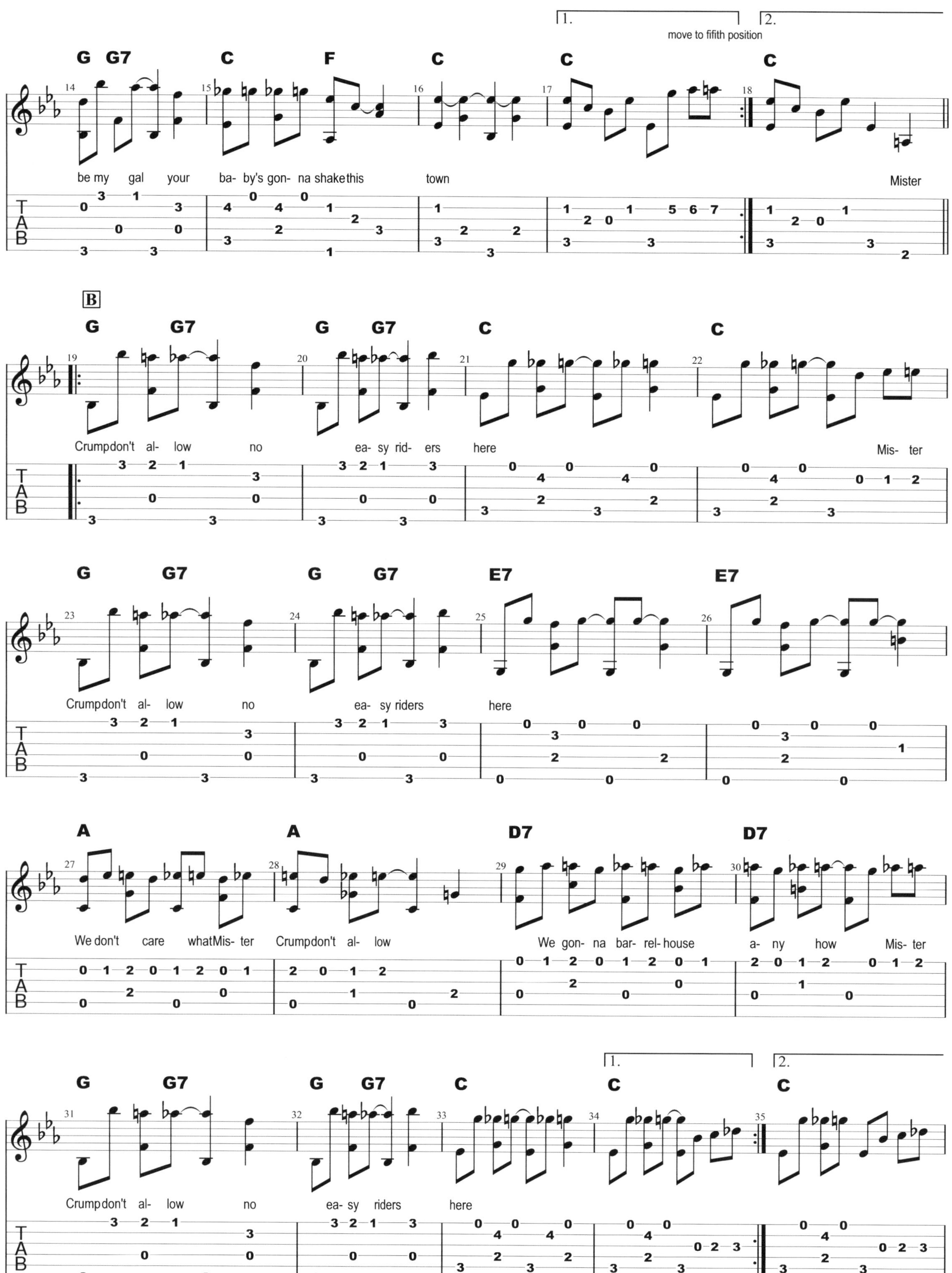
1.
2.
move to fififth position
G G7 C F C C C
be my gal your ba- by's gon- na shake this town
Mister
B
G G7 G G7 C C
Crump don't al- low no ea- sy rid- ers here
Mis- ter
G G7 G G7 E7 E7
Crump don't al- low no ea- sy riders here
A A D7 D7
We don't care what Mis- ter Crump don't al- low
We gon- na bar- rel- house a- ny how Mis- ter
G G7 G G7 C C C
Crump don't al- low no ea- sy riders here
T
A
B

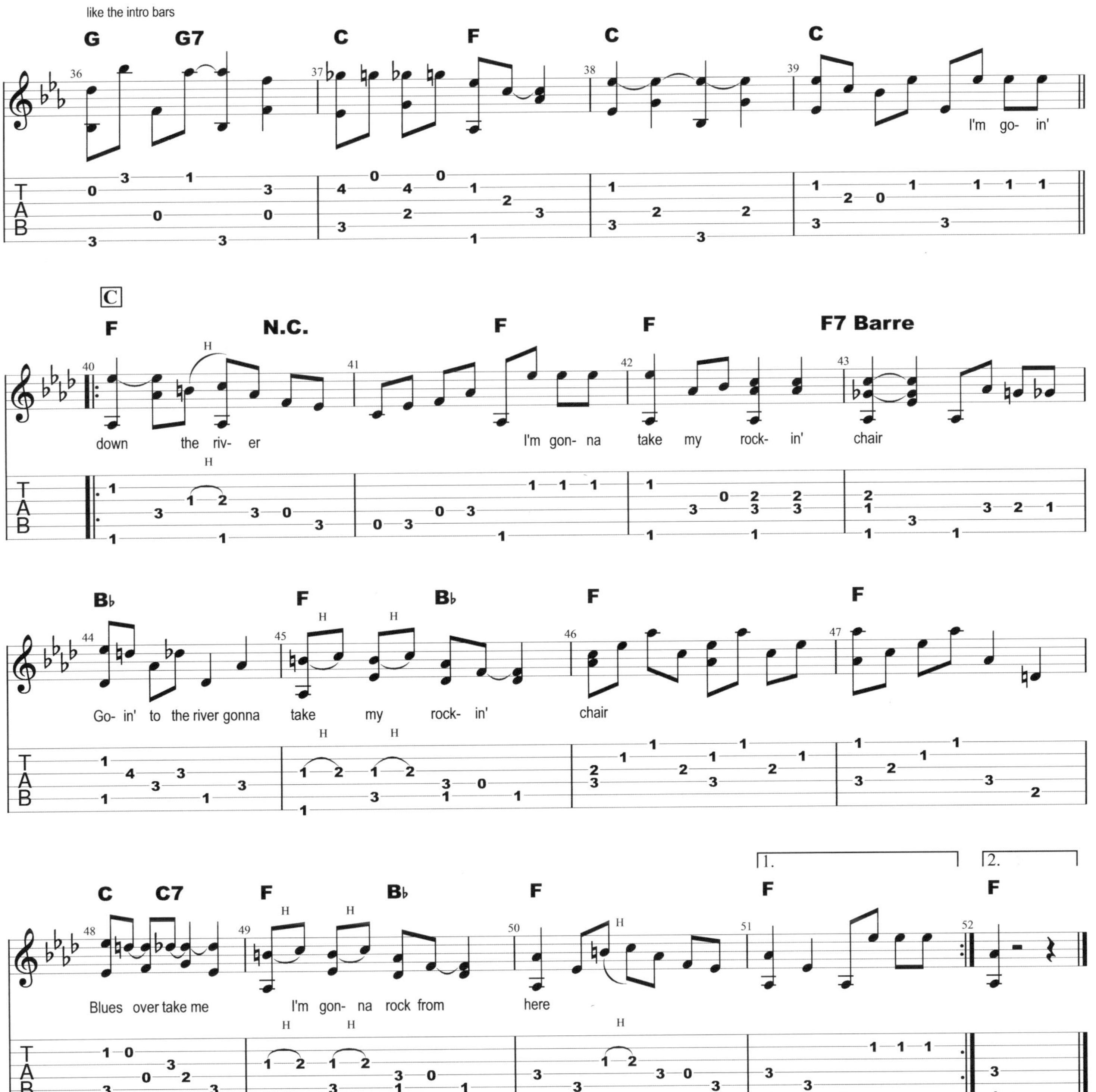

like the intro bars
G
G7
C
F
C
C
I'm go- in'
C
F
N.C.
F
F
F7 Barre
down the riv- er
I'm gon- na take my rock- in' chair
B♭
F
B♭
F
F
Go- in' to the river gonna take my rock- in' chair
1.
2.
C
C7
F
B♭
F
F
F
Blues over take me
I'm gon- na rock from here

Beale Street Blues
Written by W. C. Handy

Beale Street is the famous home of the Blues in downtown Memphis, TN. From the 1920s to the 1940s many blues and jazz legends played in the clubs there and helped develop the style known as Memphis Blues. Handy wrote the song "Beale Street Blues" in 1916, and it was published by Handy and Pace in 1917. Marion Harris had a hit with the song in 1921. If you visit Beale Street, be sure to see the statue of W. C. Handy, and visit Mr. Handy's Blues Hall, a classic "juke joint" among the variety of clubs and neon signs there today.

A

I've seen the lights of gay Broadway
Old Market Street by the Frisco Bay
I've strolled the Prado, I've gambled on the Bourse

The seven wonders of the world I've seen
And many are the places I have been
Take my advice, folks, see Beale Street first

B

You'll see pretty ladies in beautiful gowns
You'll see tailor mades and hand-me-downs
You'll meet honest men and pickpockets skilled
You'll find business never closes till someone gets killed

If Beale Street could talk, if Beale Street could talk
Married men would have to take their beds and walk
Except one or two who never drink booze
And the blind man on the corner with the Beale Street Blues

C

I'd rather be here than any place I know
I'd rather be here than any place I know
It's gonna take the sergeant for to make me go

I'm goin' to the river, here's the reason why
I'm goin' to the river and here's the reason why
Because the river's wet and Beale Street's gone dry

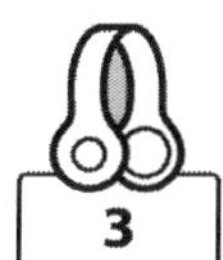

Beale Street Blues

by W. C. Handy (arranged for guitar by Jon Shain)

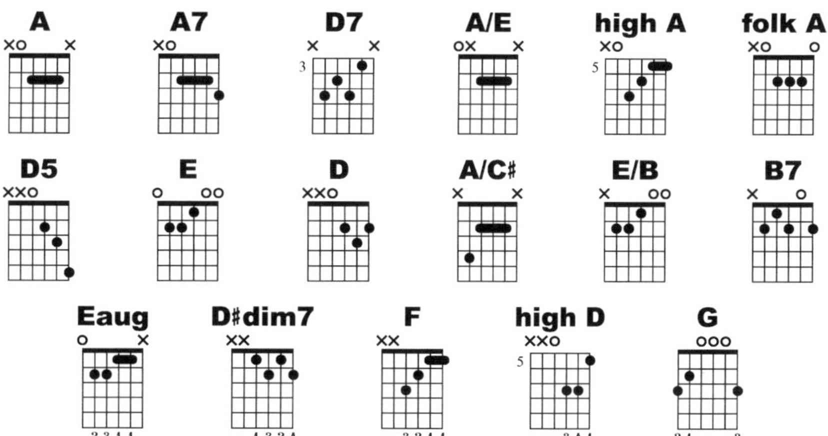

Standard tuning

♩ = 130

Intro

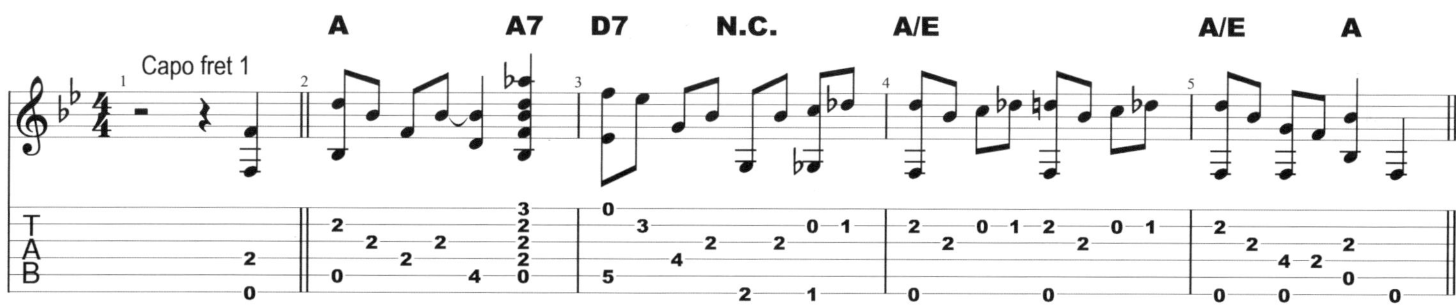

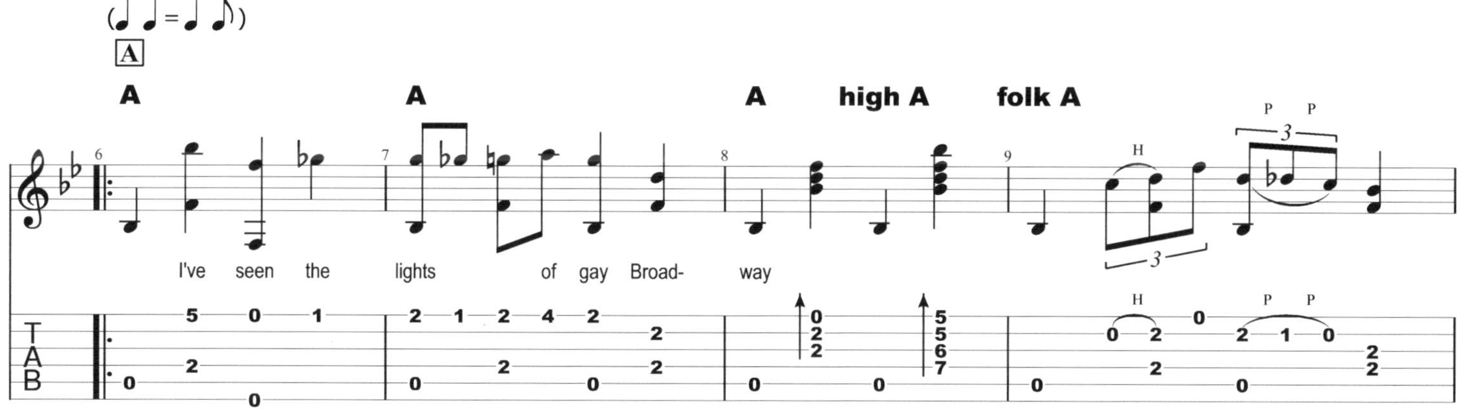

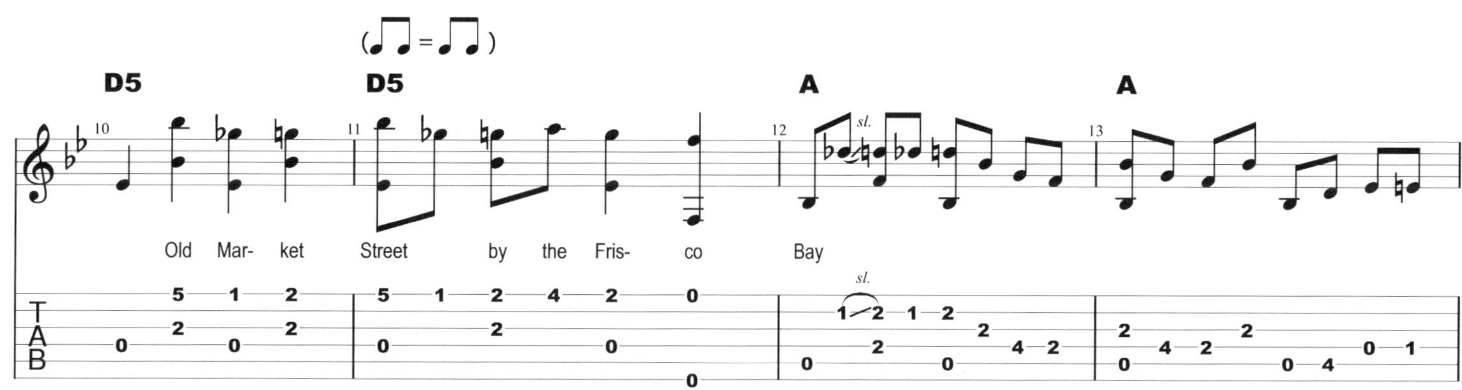

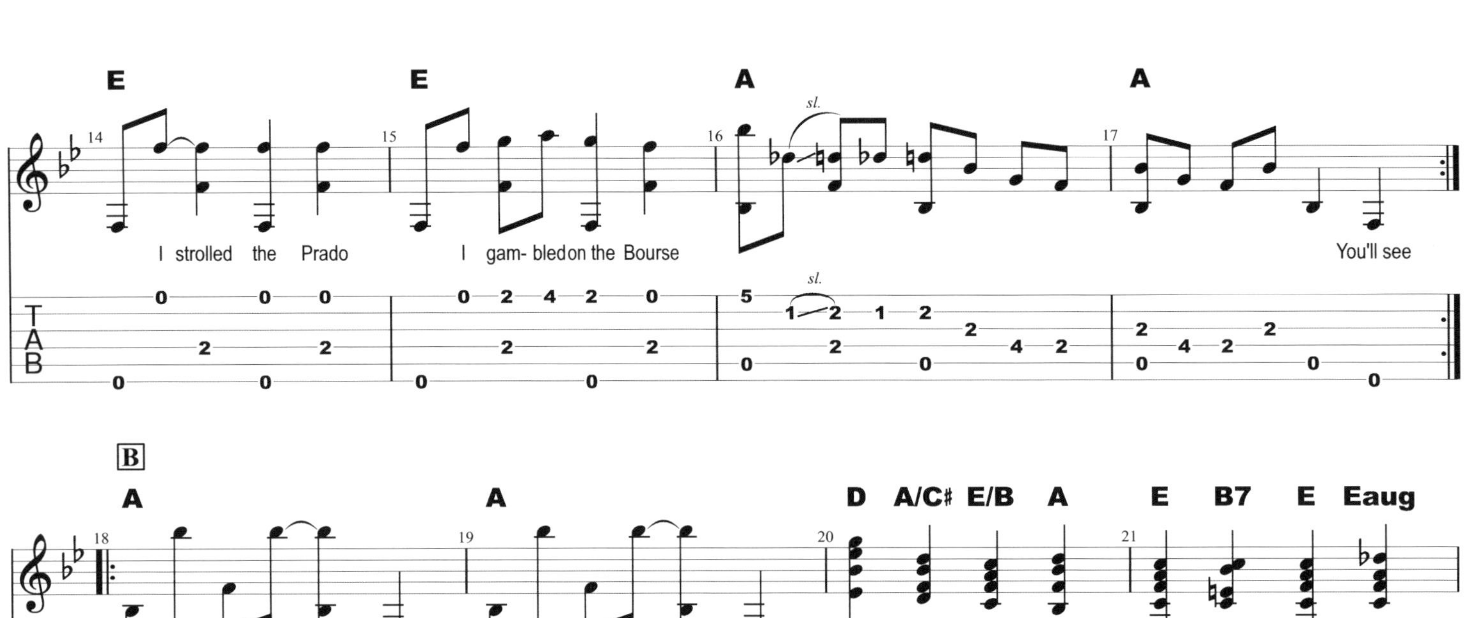
E
E
A
A
I strolled the Prado
I gambled on the Bourse
You'll see
sl.

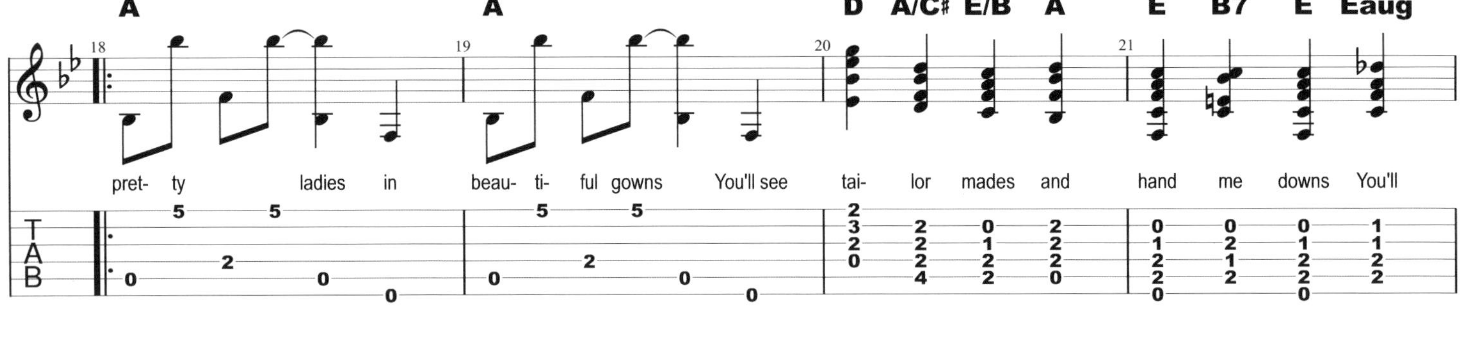
B
A
A
D A/C♯ E/B A
E B7 E Eaug
pret- ty ladies in beau- ti- ful gowns You'll see tai- lor mades and hand me downs You'll

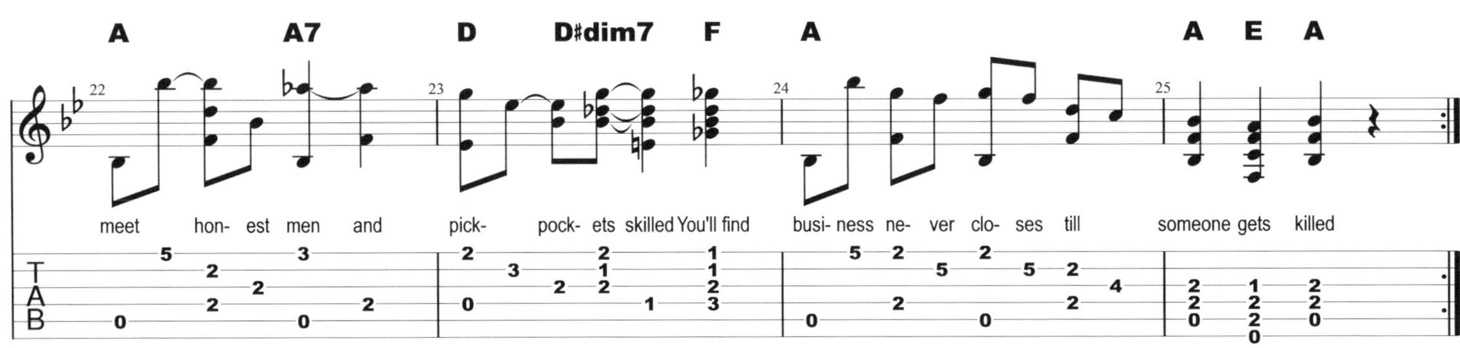
A A7 D D♯dim7 F A A E A
meet hon- est men and pick- pock- ets skilled You'll find busi- ness ne- ver clo- ses till someone gets killed

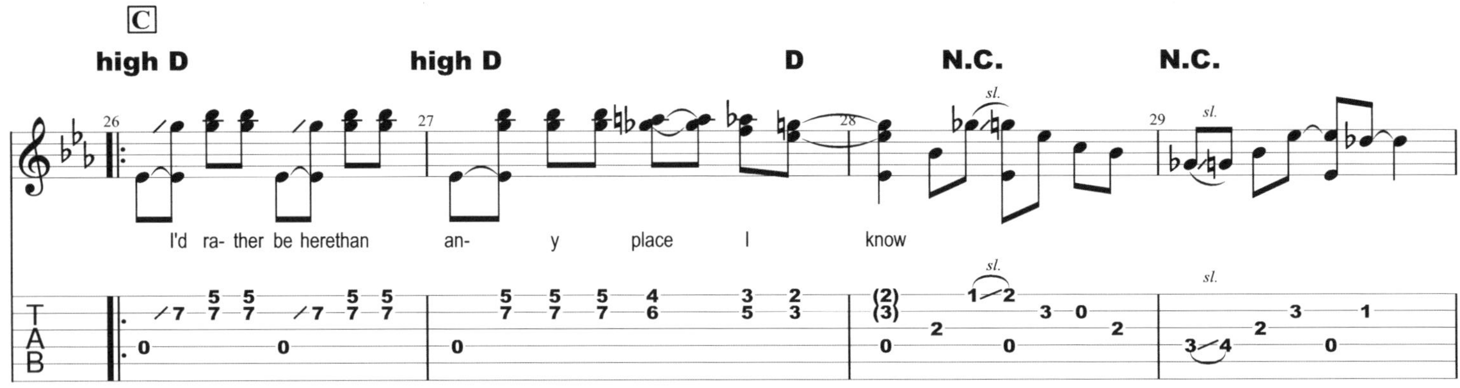
C
high D
high D
D
N.C.
N.C.
I'd ra- ther be here than an- y place I know
sl.

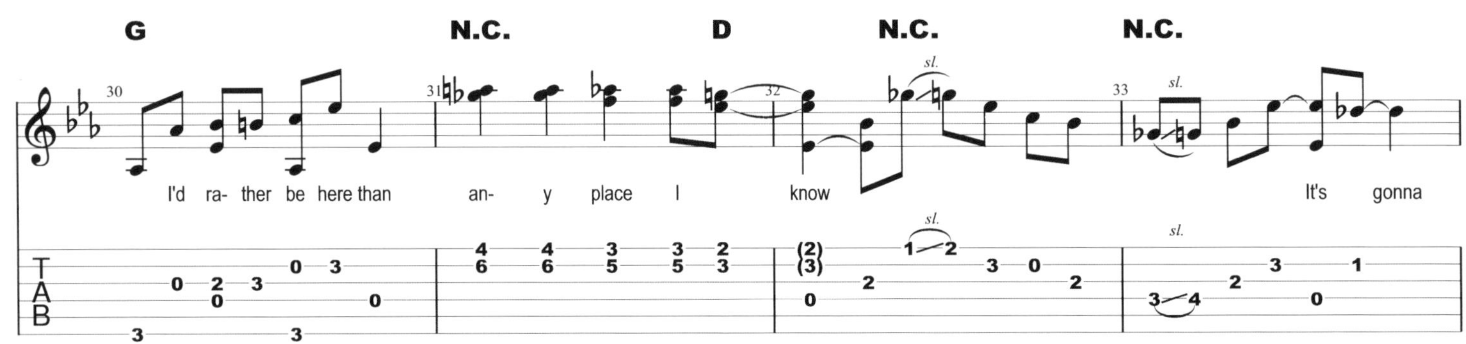
G
N.C.
D
N.C.
N.C.
I'd ra- ther be here than an- y place I know
It's gonna
sl.

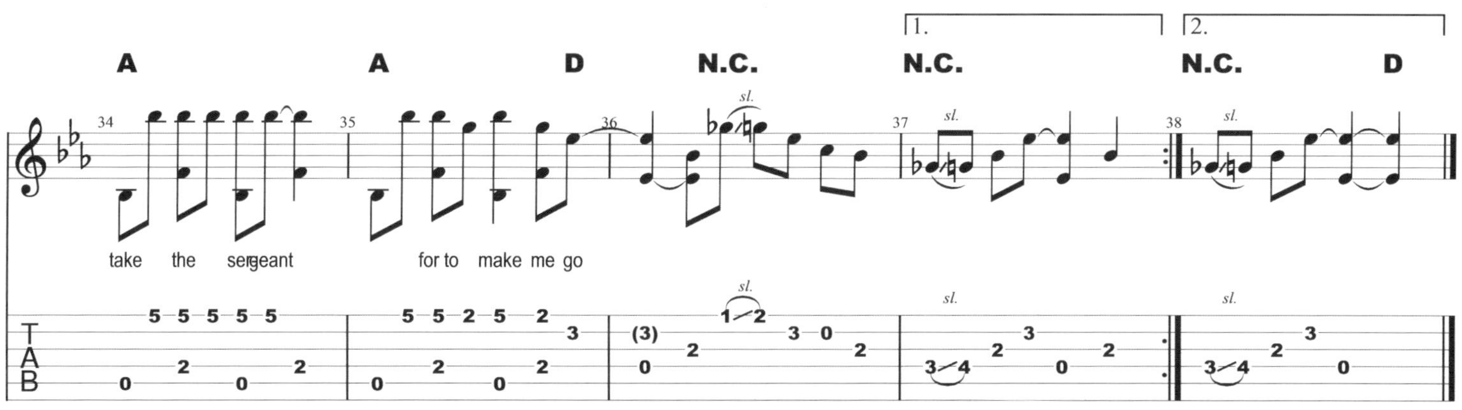

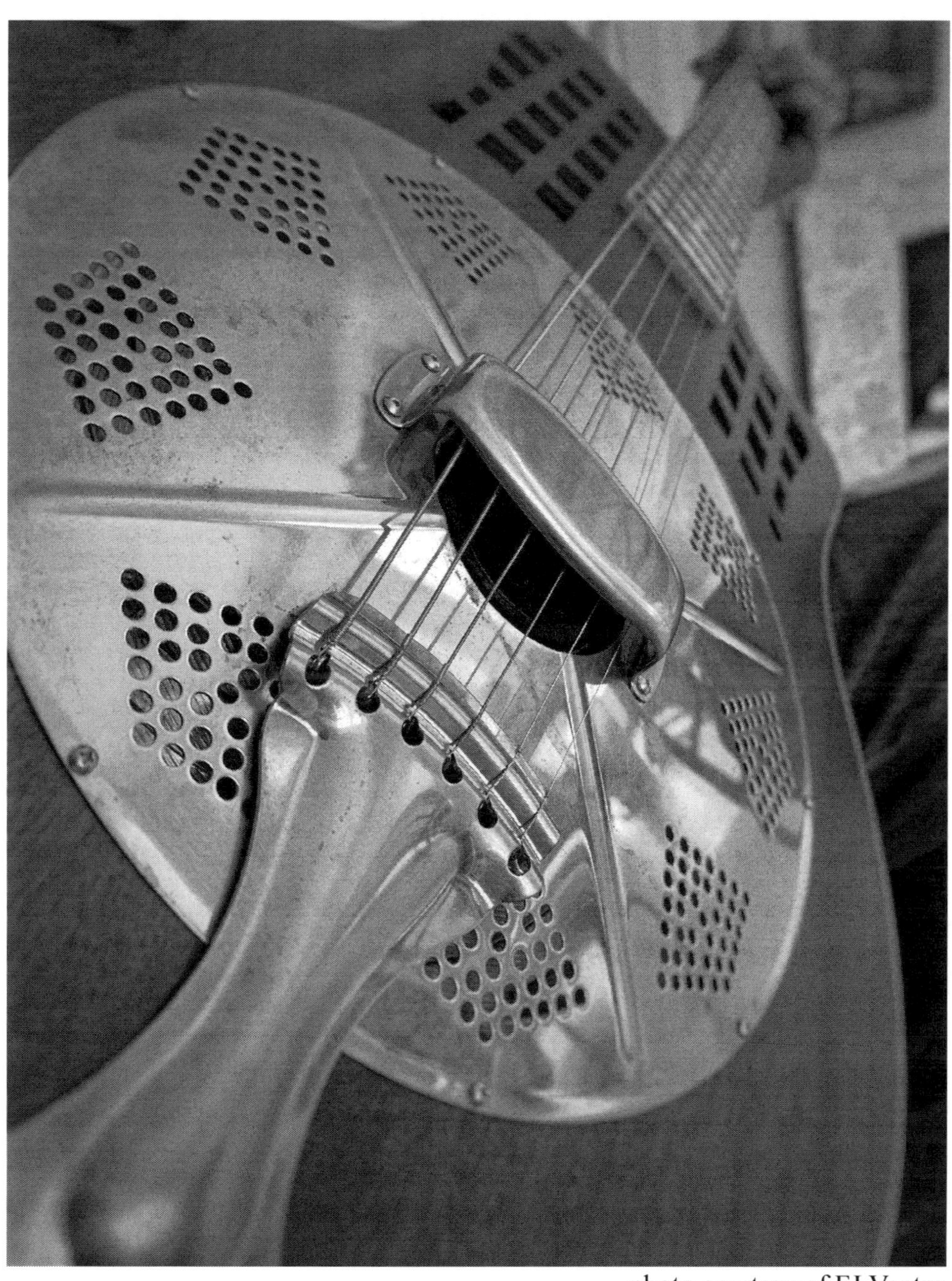
photo courtesy of FJ Ventre

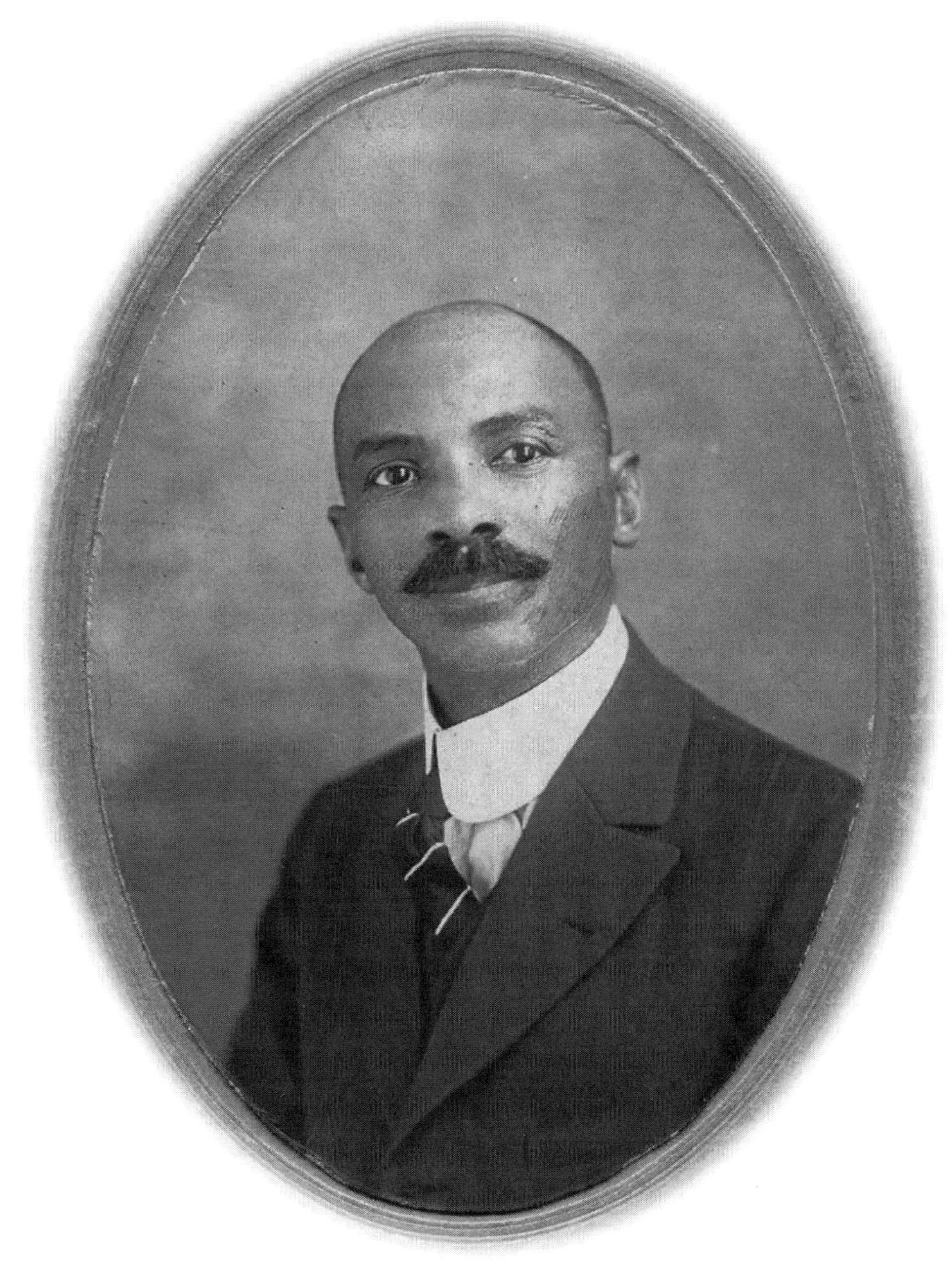

W. C. Handy

Aunt Hagar's Children Blues

Written by W. C. Handy and J. Tim Brymn

On a trip to Chicago in 1920, an idea for a song came to Handy and he wrote it quickly. His memoir isn't clear as to whether he wrote it at a barber shop or on the train. Handy's mother had occasionally referred to the African American community as "Aunt Hagar's children". Hagar, as you may remember from the bible story, was the mother of Ishmael, Abraham's first son, discarded and exiled along with his mother after Isaac was born. "Aunt Hagar's Children Blues" captures a look into the Black church and its relationship to music. I leaned heavily on Louis Armstrong's version of this tune for its rhythmic cadence. The original by Handy's big band is much faster and instrumental only.

A

Old Deacon Splivin, his flock was given the way of livin', livin' right
Said he no wingin', no ragtime singin' tonight
Up jumped Aunt Hagar, she shouted out with all her might

B

She said, oh, 'tain't no use in preachin', oh, 'tain't no use in teachin'
Each modulation of syncopation just tell my feet to dance and I can't refuse
When I hear the melody called the Blues, those ever-lovin' Blues

C

Just hear Aunt Hagar's children harmonizin' to that old mournful tune
It's like a choir from on high broke loose
And if the devil brought it, the good Lord he sent it right down to me
Let the congregation join while I sing those lovin' Aunt Hagar's Blues

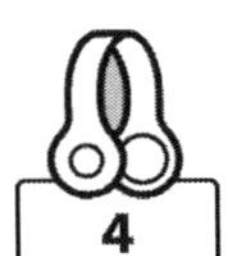

Aunt Hagar's Children Blues

by W. C. Handy and J. Tim Brymn (arranged for guitar by Jon Shain)

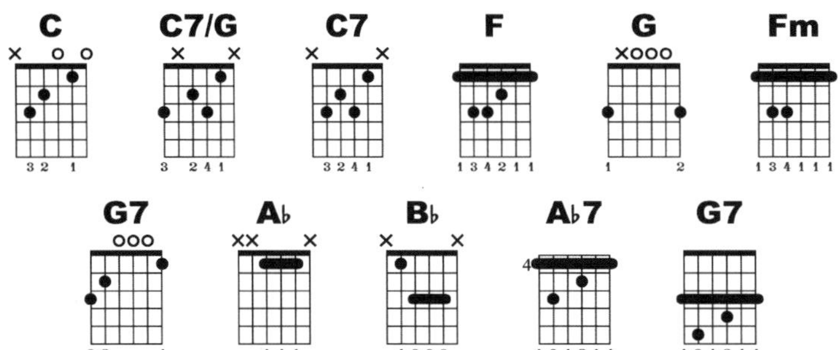

Standard tuning

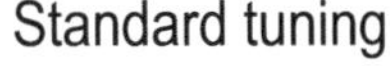

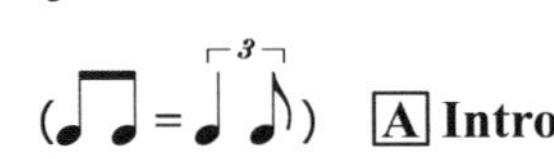

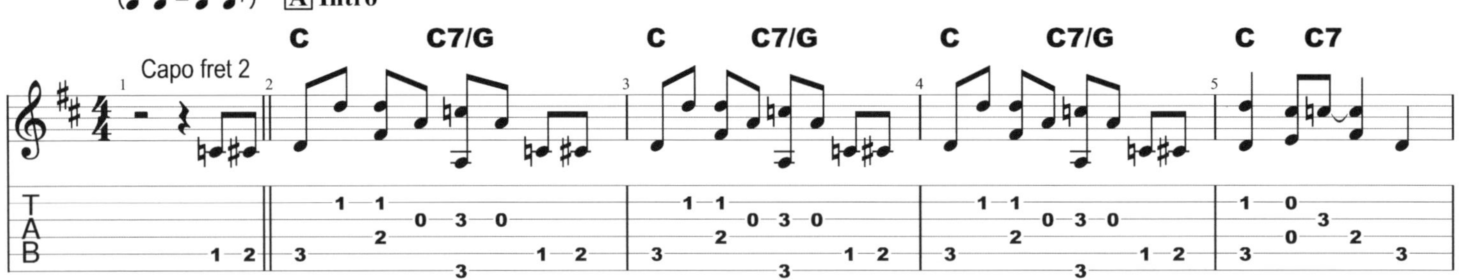

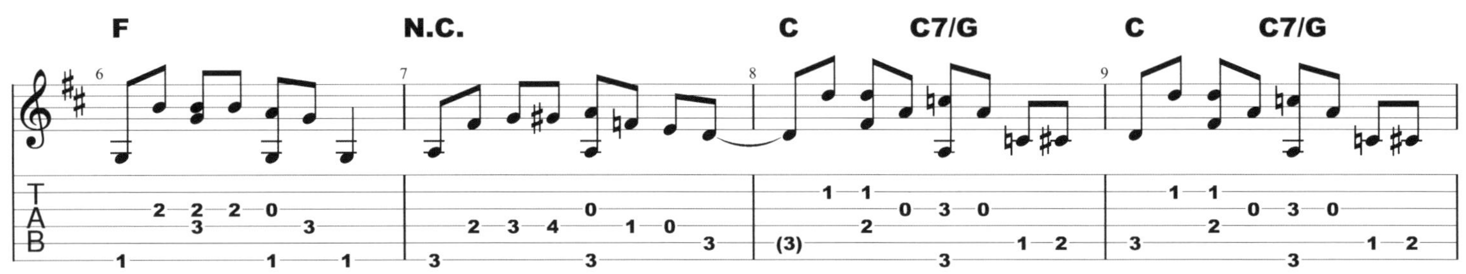

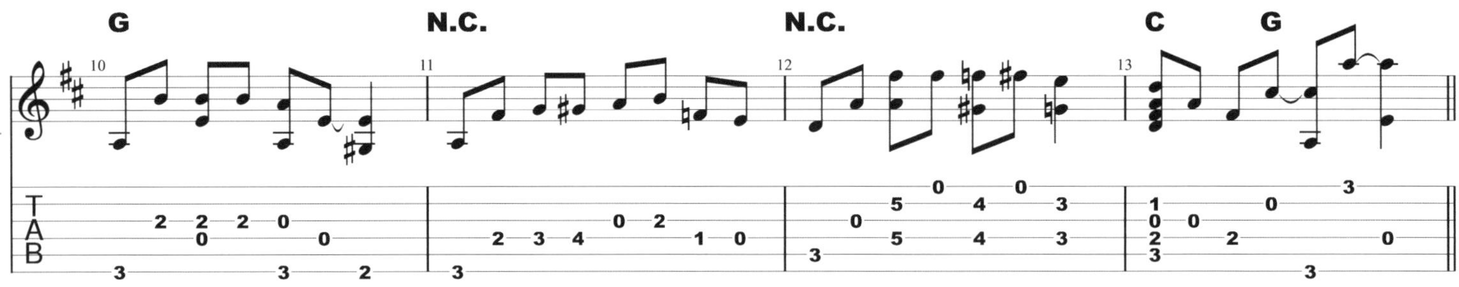

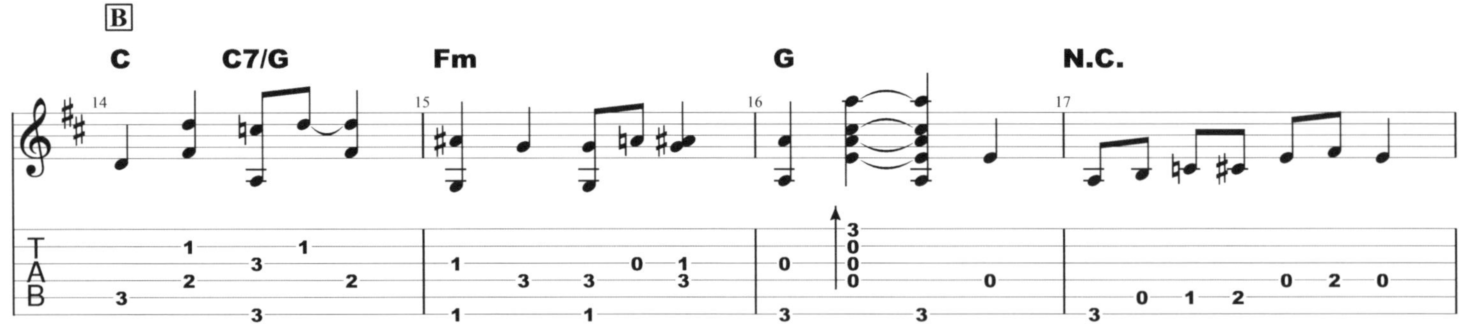

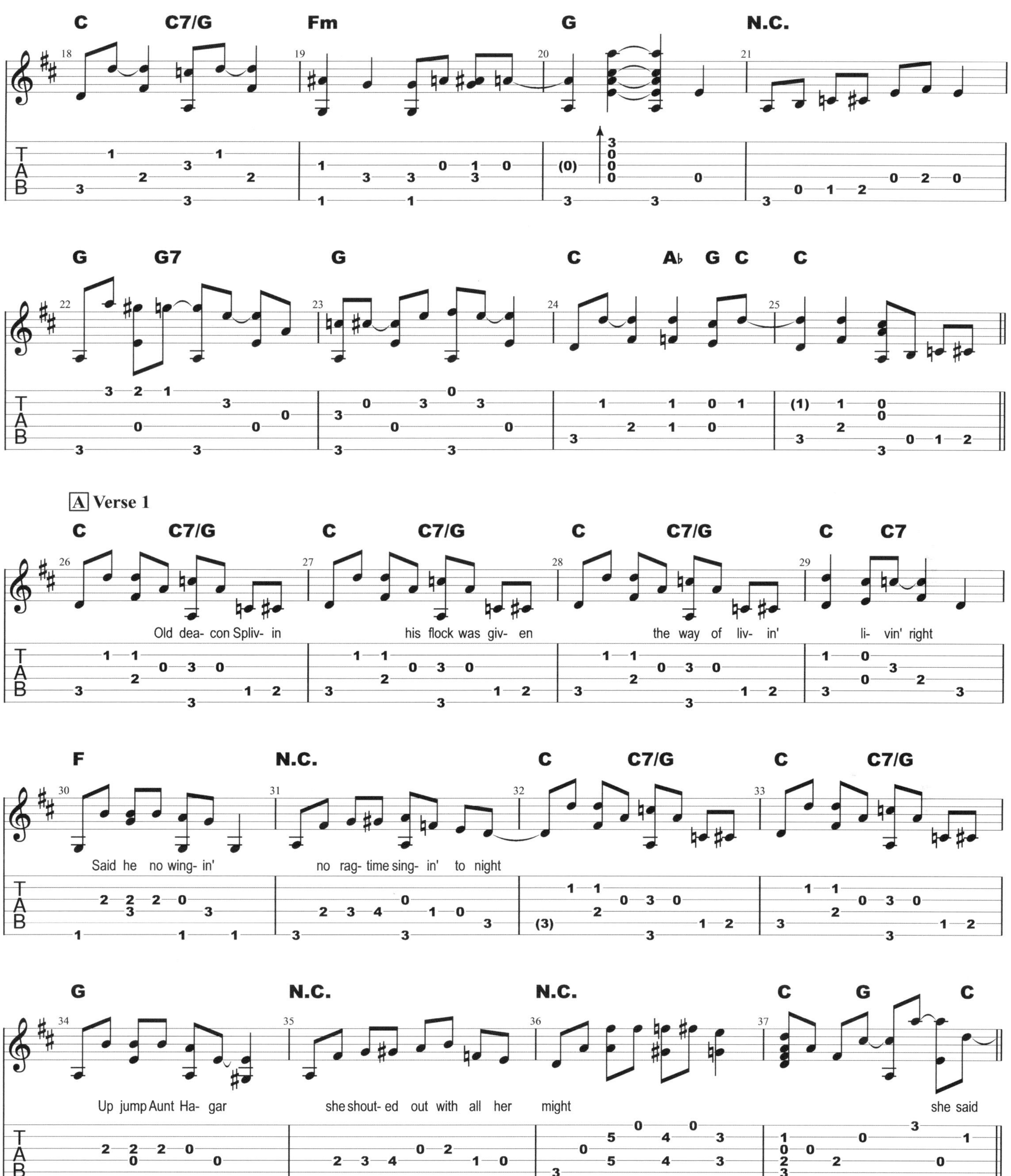
C C7/G Fm G N.C.
G G7 G C A♭ G C C
A Verse 1
C C7/G C C7/G C C7/G C C7
Old dea- con Spliv- in his flock was giv- en the way of liv- in' li- vin' right
F N.C. C C7/G C C7/G
Said he no wing- in' no rag- time sing- in' to night
G N.C. N.C. C G C
Up jump Aunt Ha- gar she shout- ed out with all her might she said

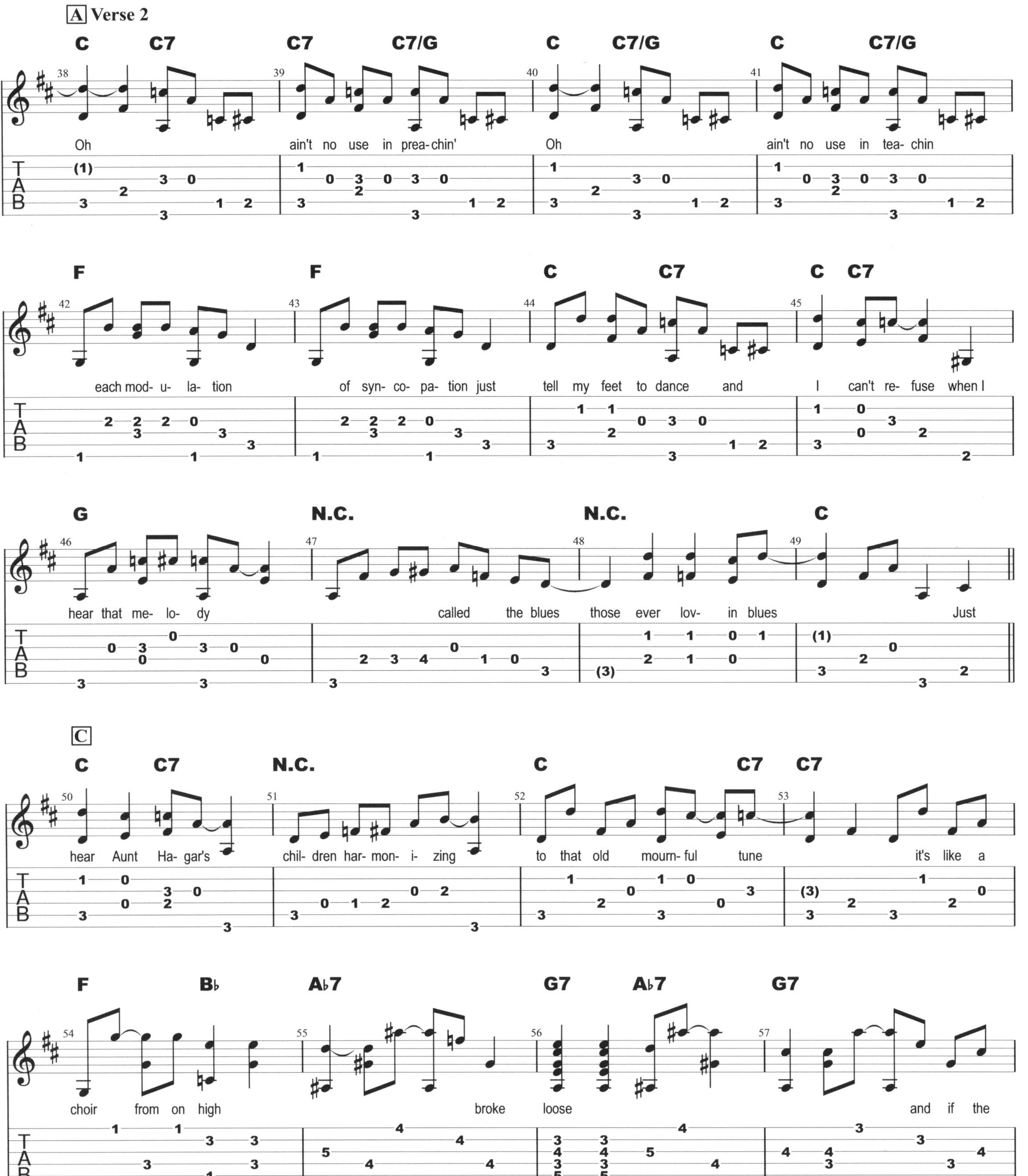
A Verse 2
C C7 C7 C7/G C C7/G C C7/G
Oh ain't no use in prea-chin' Oh ain't no use in tea-chin
F F C C7 C C7
each mod- u- la- tion of syn- co- pa- tion just tell my feet to dance and I can't re- fuse when I
G N.C. N.C. C
hear that me- lo- dy called the blues those ever lov- in blues Just
C
C C7 N.C. C C7 C7
hear Aunt Ha- gar's chil- dren har- mon- i- zing to that old mourn- ful tune it's like a
F B♭ A♭7 G7 A♭7 G7
choir from on high broke loose and if the

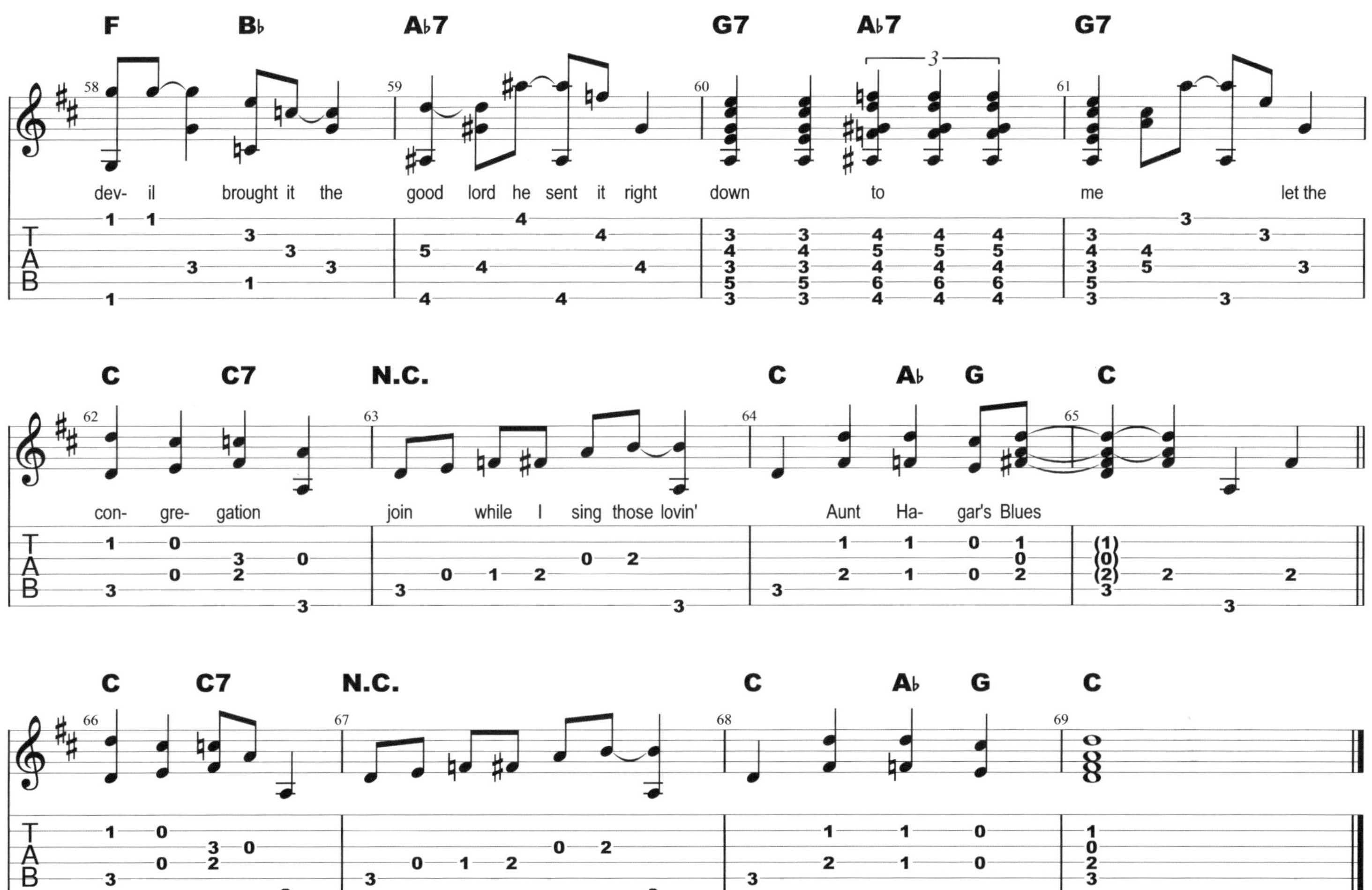
F Bb Ab7 G7 Ab7 G7
dev- il brought it the good lord he sent it right down to me let the
C C7 N.C. C Ab G C
con- gre- gation join while I sing those lovin' Aunt Ha- gar's Blues
C C7 N.C. C Ab G C

Joe Turner Blues

Written by W. C. Handy

Although Handy wrote "Joe Turner Blues" in 1914 and published it a year later, Joe Turner was a popular figure in folk songs as far back as the 1890's. The older folk song Joe Turner was considered to be inspired by Joe Turney, a notorious lawman who gathered up and imprisoned many Black men in rural Tennessee, selling their labor for profit. In Handy's version of the Joe Turner story, the music stayed in place, but as in many folk songs, the lyrics became much more palatable to the general public when it was sold as a "popular" song. And so, we now have Joe Turner presented as a sympathetic character who considers himself the victim in a broken-hearted love-sick blues.

A

You'll never miss the water till your well runs dry
Till your well runs dry
You'll never miss Joe Turner till he says goodbye

Sweet babe I'm gonna leave you and the time ain't long
No, the time ain't long
If you don't believe I'm leavin', count the days I'm gone

B

You will be sorry, sorry from your heart, mmm, mmm
Sorry to your heart
Some day when you and I must part

And every time you hear that whistle blow
Hear that steamboat blow
You'll hate the day that you lost your Joe

A

I bought a bulldog for to watch you while you sleep
Guard you while you sleep
I spent all my money, now you call Joe Turner cheap

You never appreciate the little things I do
Not one thing I do
And that's the very reason why I'm leavin' you

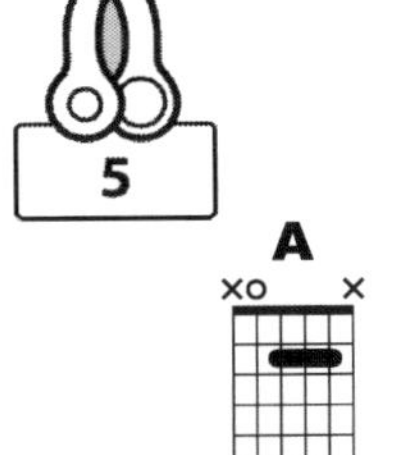

Joe Turner Blues

by W. C. Handy (arranged for guitar by Jon Shain)

A E A7 D7 Am/D E7 D Dsus2 D7/F♯

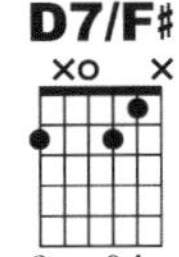

Standard tuning

♩ = 78

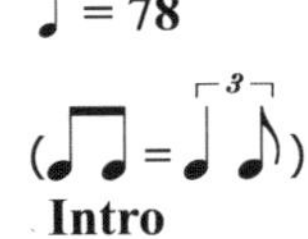

Intro

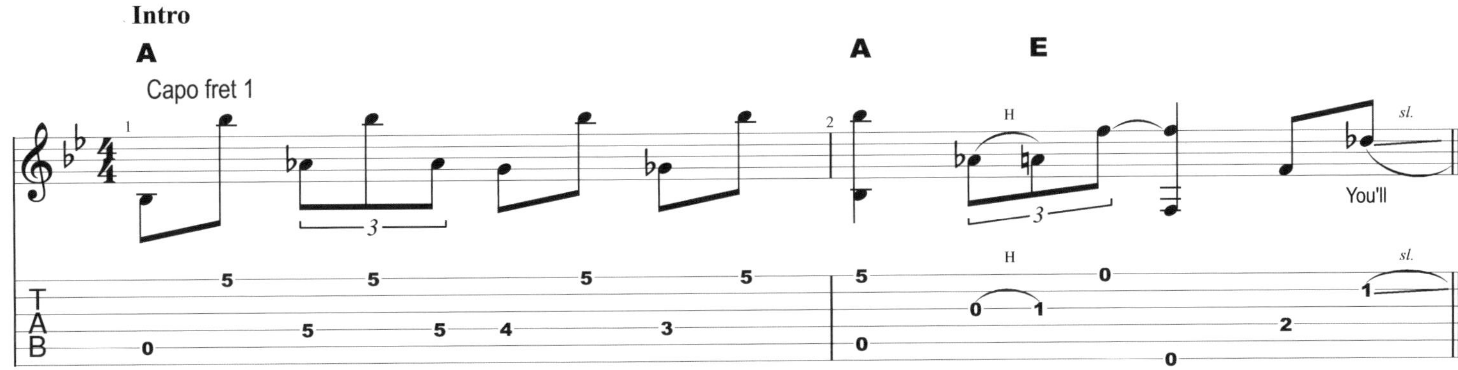

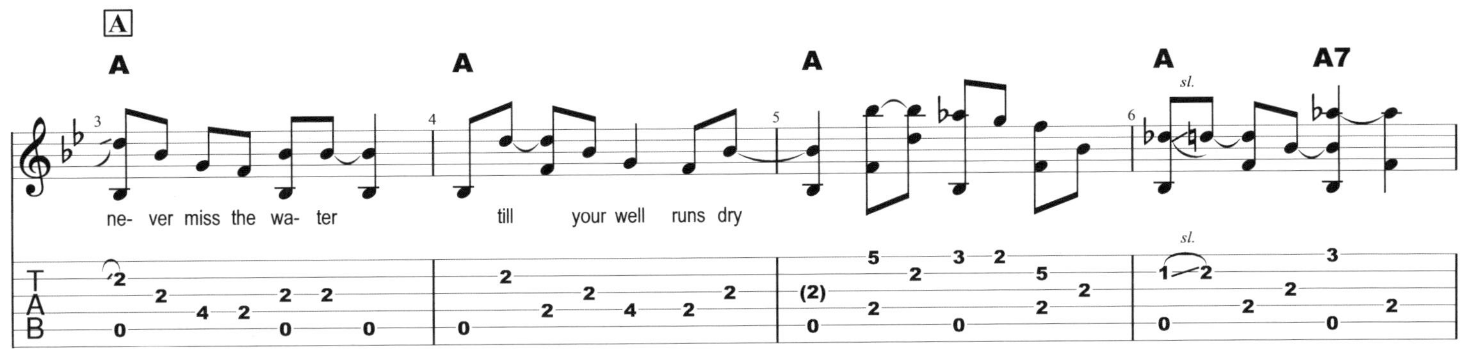

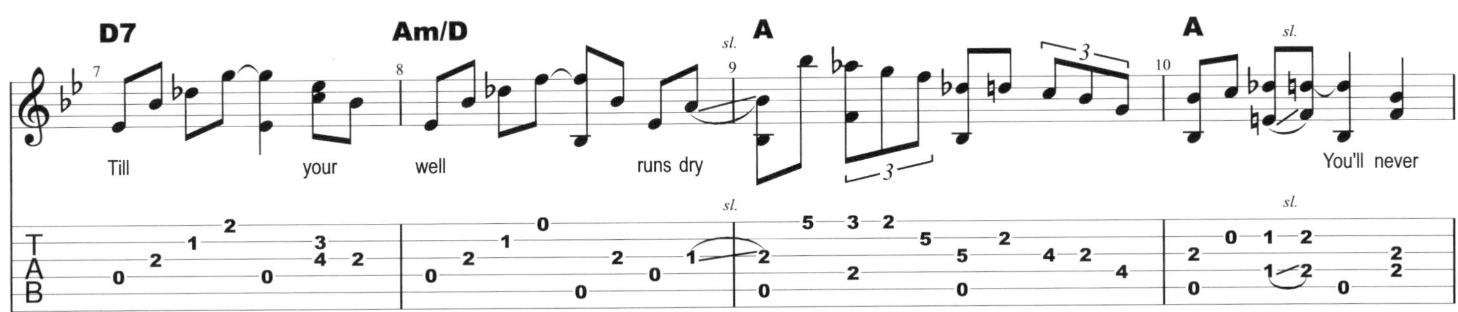

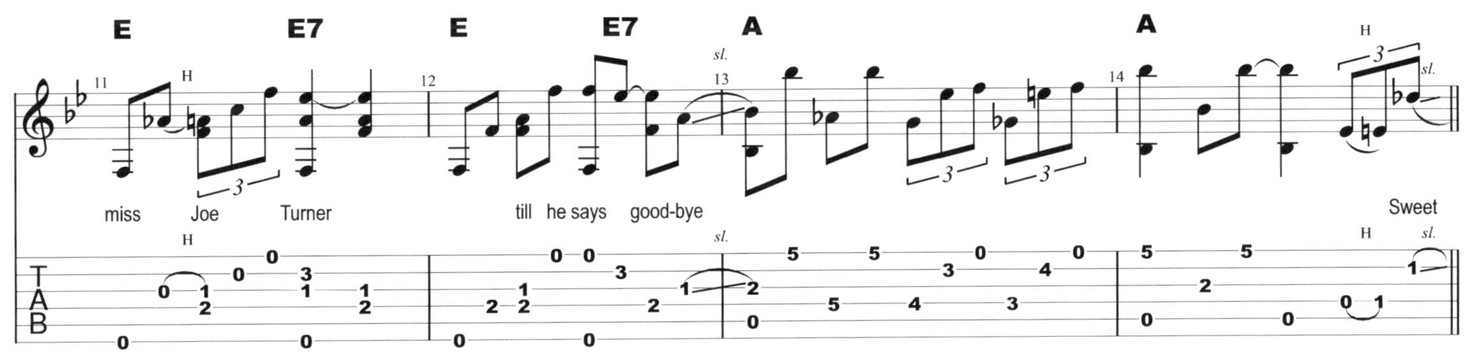

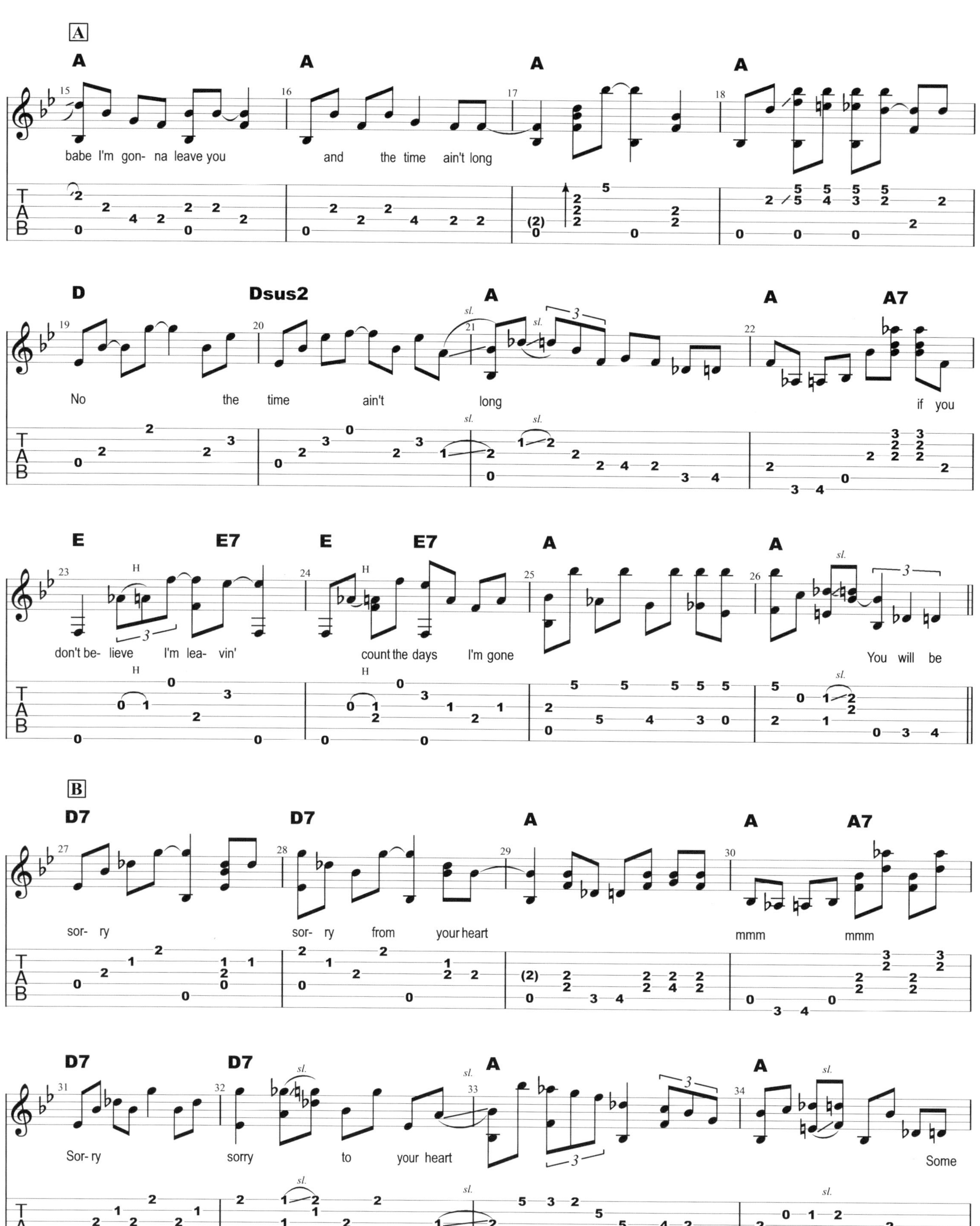
A
A A A A
babe I'm gon- na leave you
and the time ain't long
D Dsus2 A A A7
No the time ain't long if you
E E7 E E7 A A
don't be- lieve I'm lea- vin' count the days I'm gone You will be
B
D7 D7 A A A7
sor- ry sor- ry from your heart mmm mmm
D7 D7 A A
Sor- ry sorry to your heart Some

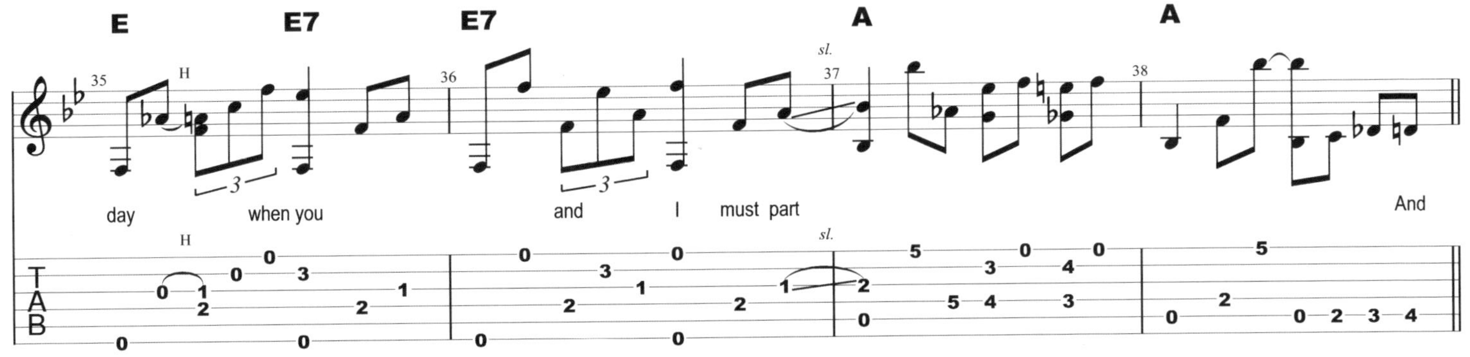
E
E7
E7
A
A
day
when you
and
I
must part
And

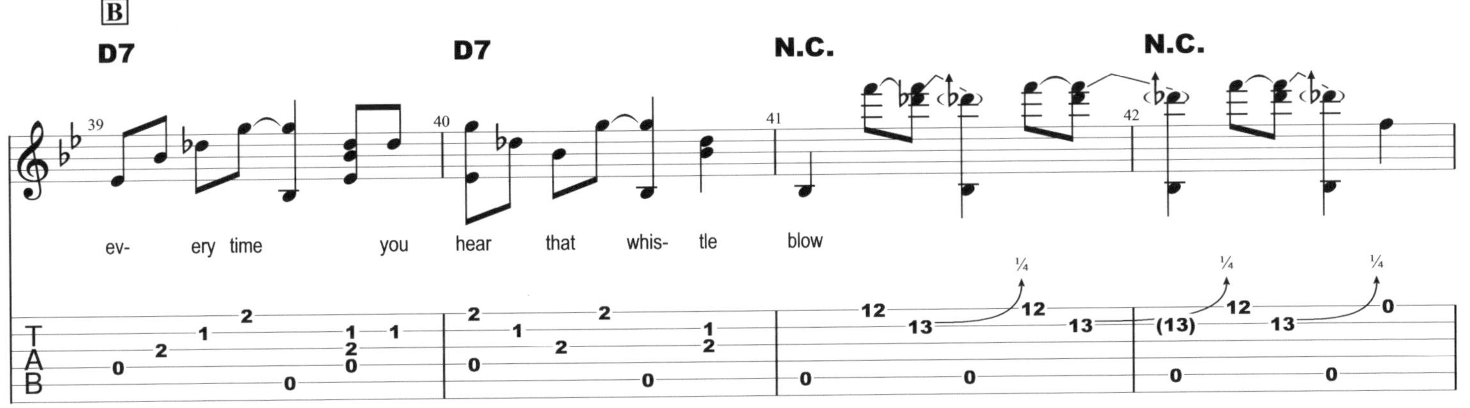
B
D7
D7
N.C.
N.C.
ev-
ery time
you
hear
that
whis-
tle
blow

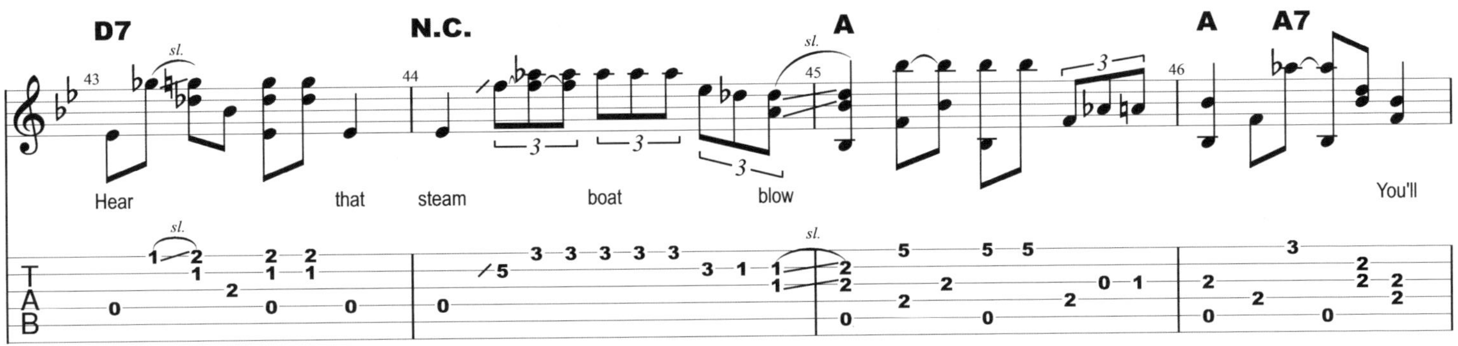
D7
N.C.
A
A
A7
Hear
that
steam
boat
blow
You'll

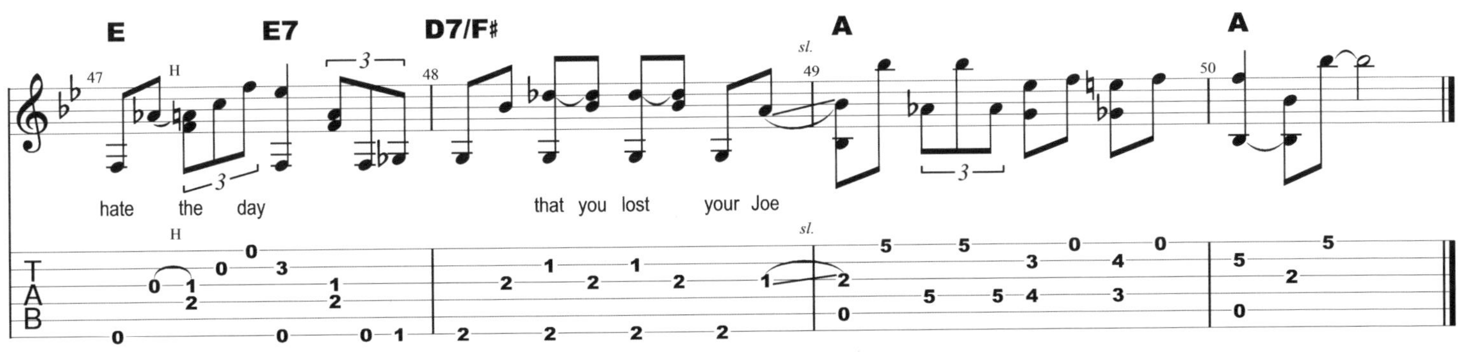
E
E7
D7/F#
A
A
hate
the
day
that you
lost
your Joe

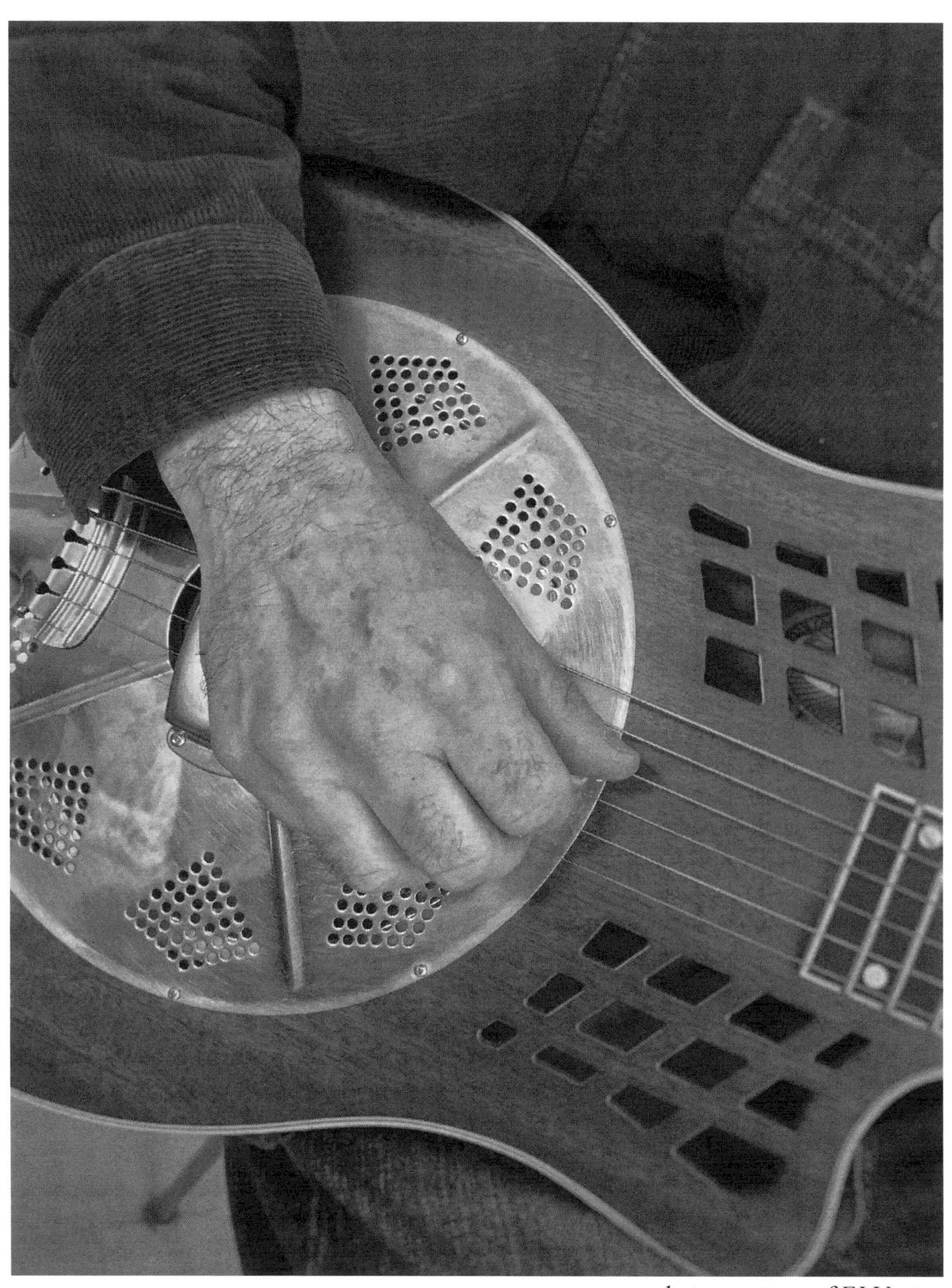

photo courtesy of FJ Ventre

Fuzzy Wuzzy Rag

In September 1917, Columbia Records brought Handy and his band to New York to record a series of wax cylinder cuts, the recording medium of the day. Here is how Handy described the recording session in his memoir:

"Our clarinetist sat on a 6-foot tall stool and played into a megaphone above him near the ceiling. There were stools of varying heights for the other players. The three violins stood directly in front of the recording apparatus and played into a megaphone there. The saxophonists were seated along a side wall and played into their own megaphones. Cornet and trombone played into one at the rear. The cellist occupied another corner and another megaphone. But the poor drummer was a dead goose where the records were concerned. While they played as hard as ever in life, the drums and basses could not be recorded in those days. All megaphones emptied into one recording horn".

Handy and his band became the second African American band to be recorded in American history, preceded only by Wilbur Sweatman in April 1917.

One of the records that W. C. Handy's band made for Columbia during that session was the only song written by a man named Al Morton. His song had been published by Pace and Handy in 1915, and it was called "Fuzzy Wuzzy Rag".

You may pick up on some phrases that are reminiscent of Scott Joplin's "Maple Leaf Rag", which was one of the most popular of the ragtime hits. Handy's recorded version of "Fuzzy Wuzzy Rag" features a ragtime orchestra playing at breakneck speeds. This song was a bear to translate to a playable version on the guitar, but it remains for me a really fun song to perform live.

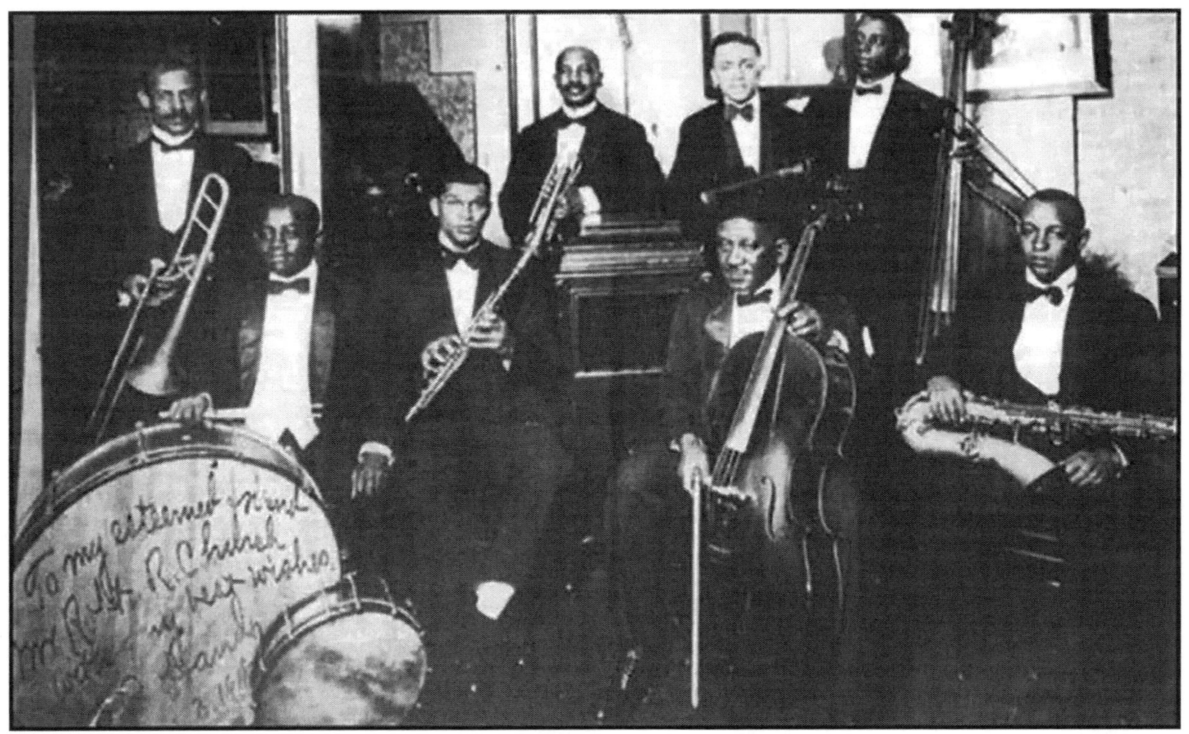

W. C. Handy Orchestra

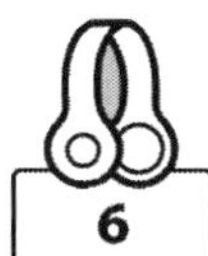

Fuzzy Wuzzy Rag

by W. C. Handy (guitar arrangement by Jon Shain)

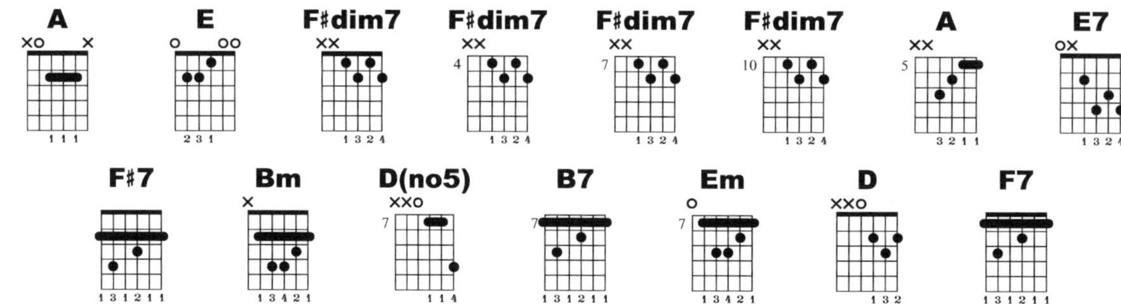

Standard tuning

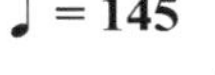

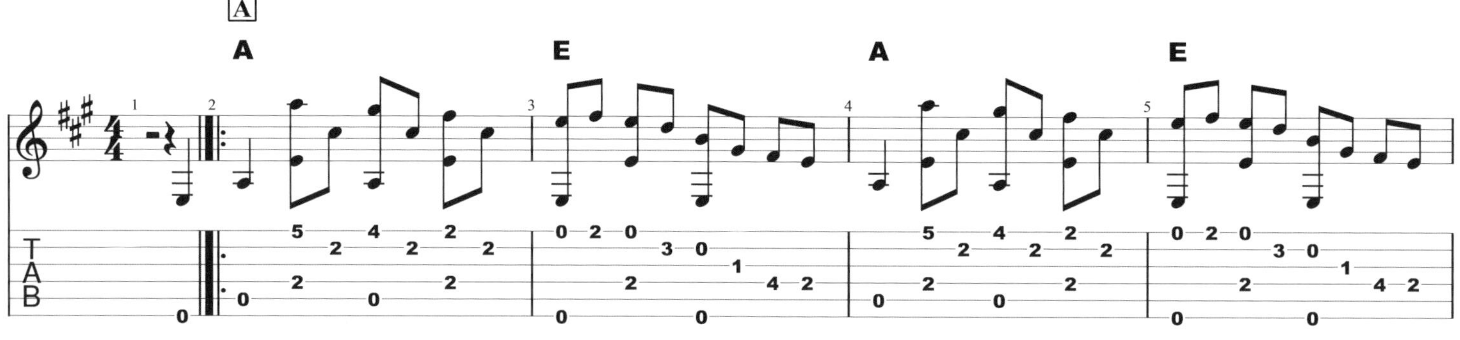

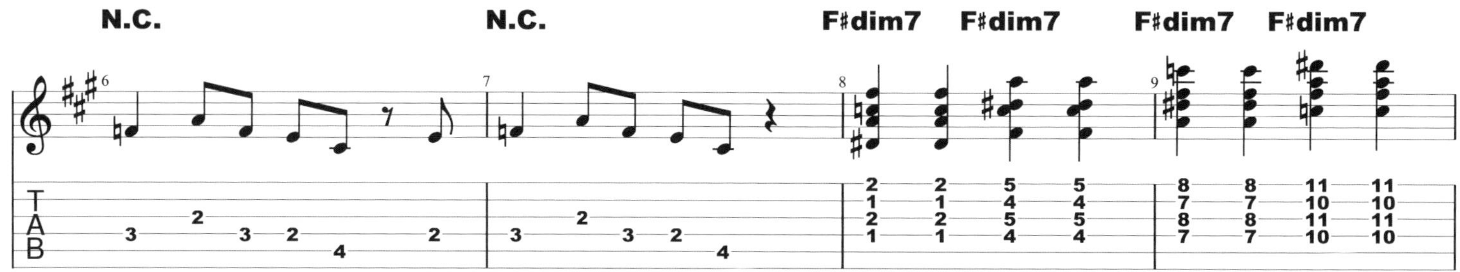

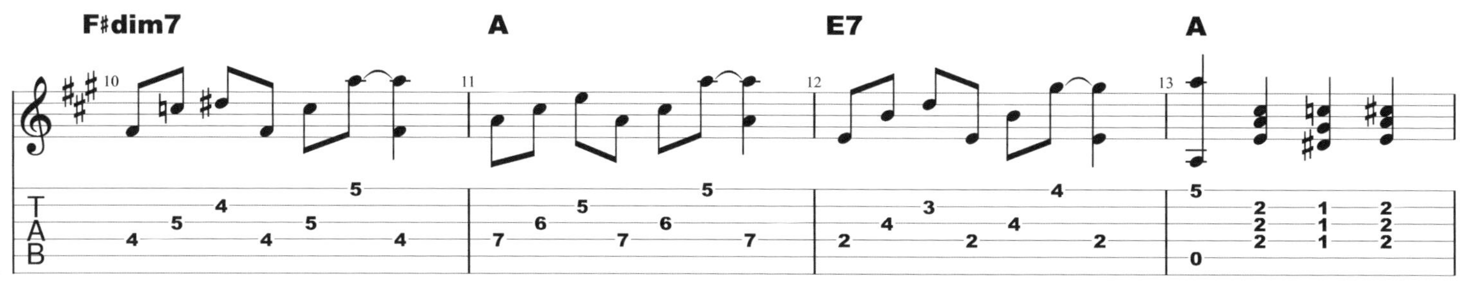

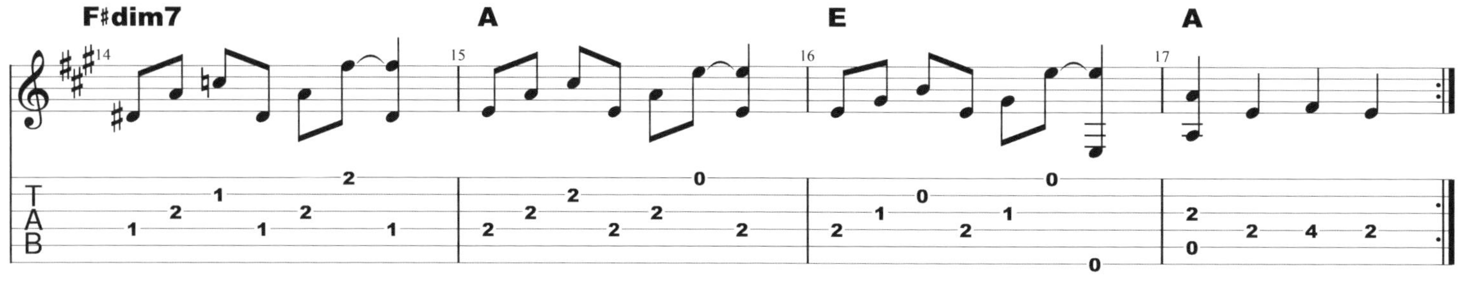

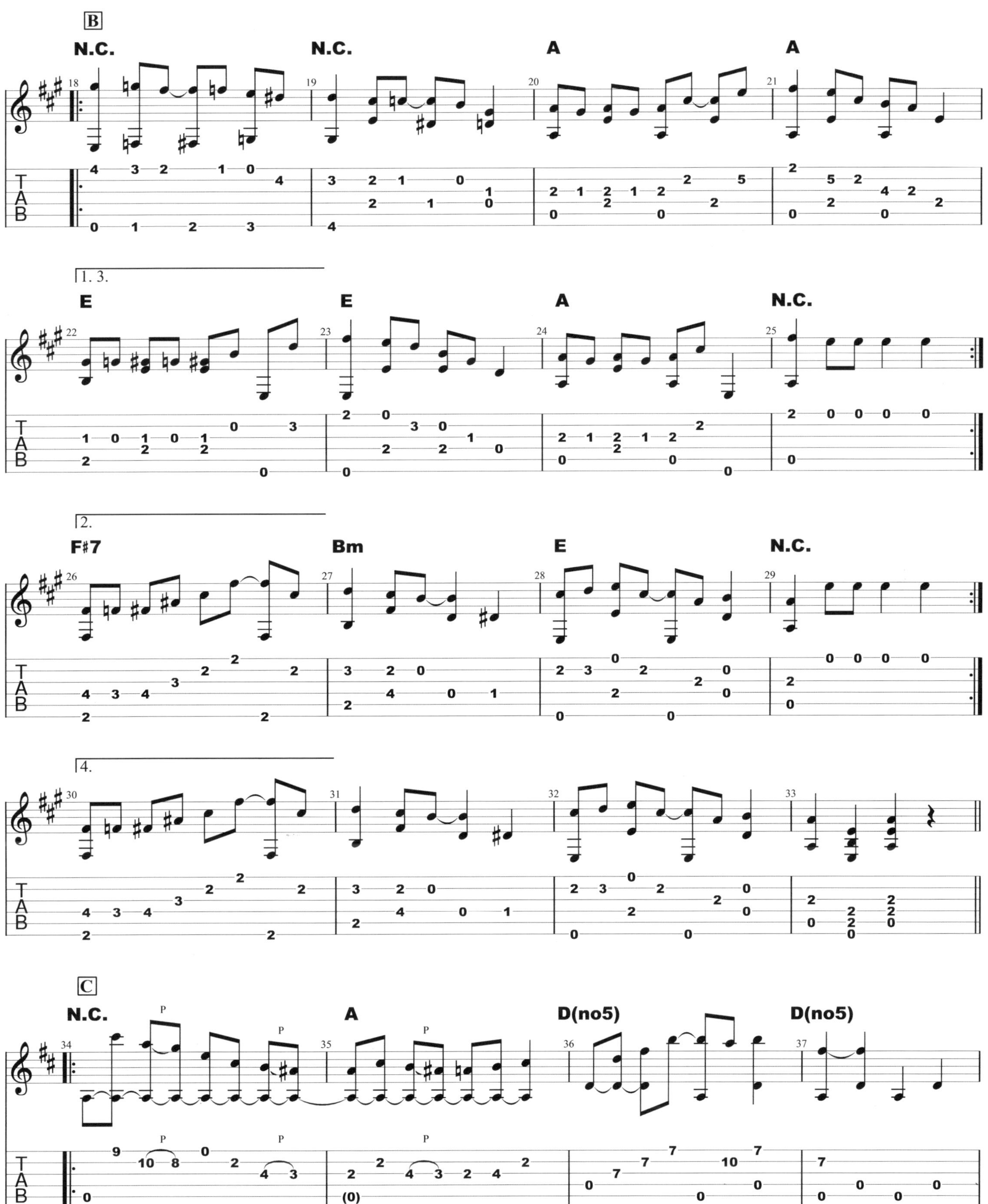
B
N.C.
N.C.
A
A
1. 3.
E
E
A
N.C.
2.
F#7
Bm
E
N.C.
4.
C
N.C.
A
D(no5)
D(no5)
P
T
A
B

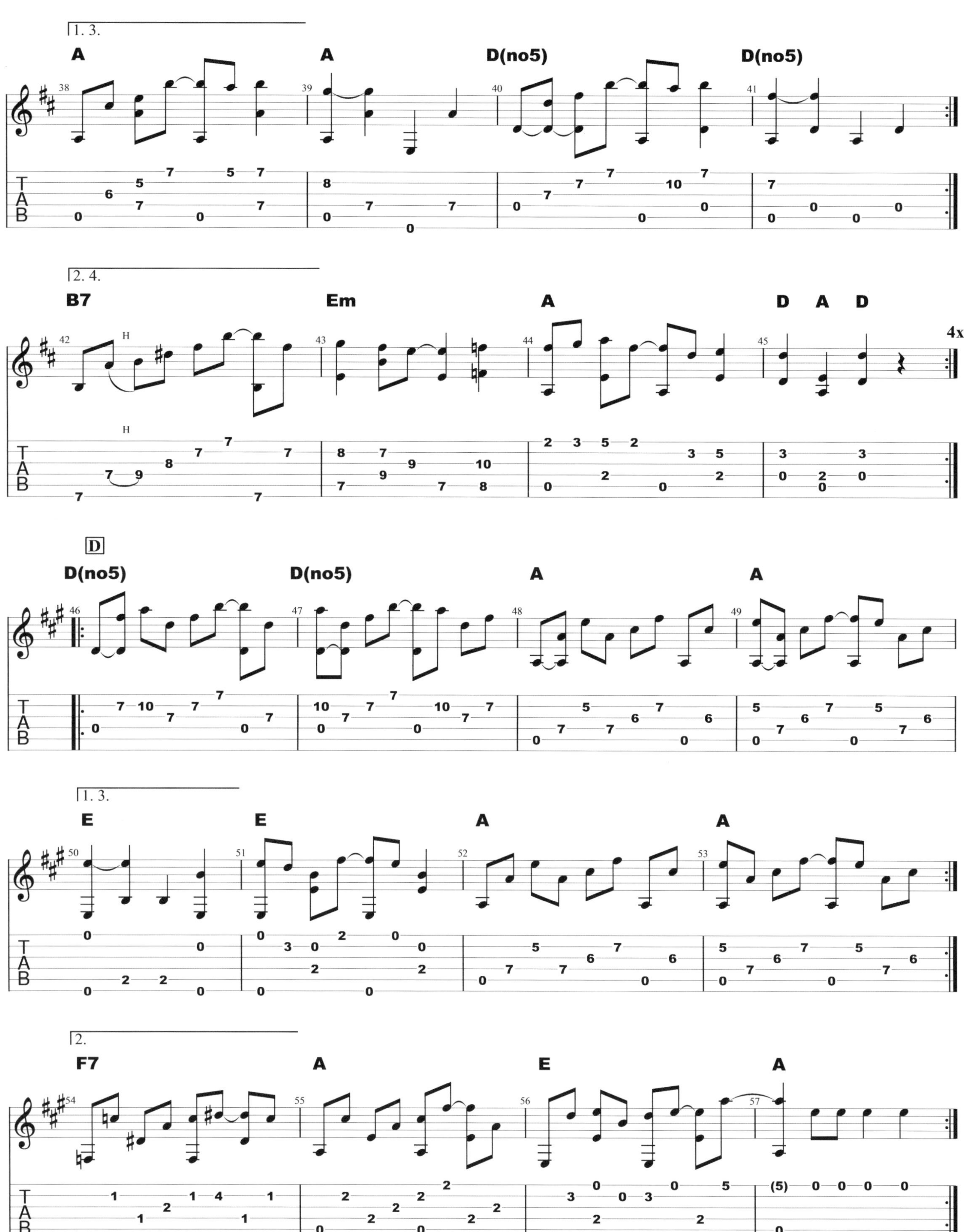
1. 3.
A
A
D(no5)
D(no5)
2. 4.
B7
Em
A
D A D
4x
D
D(no5)
D(no5)
A
A
1. 3.
E
E
A
A
2.
F7
A
E
A

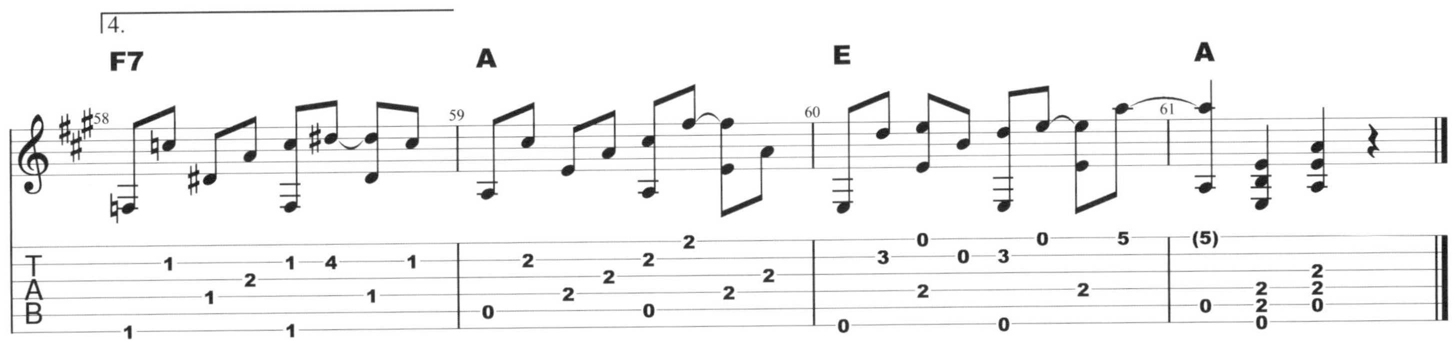

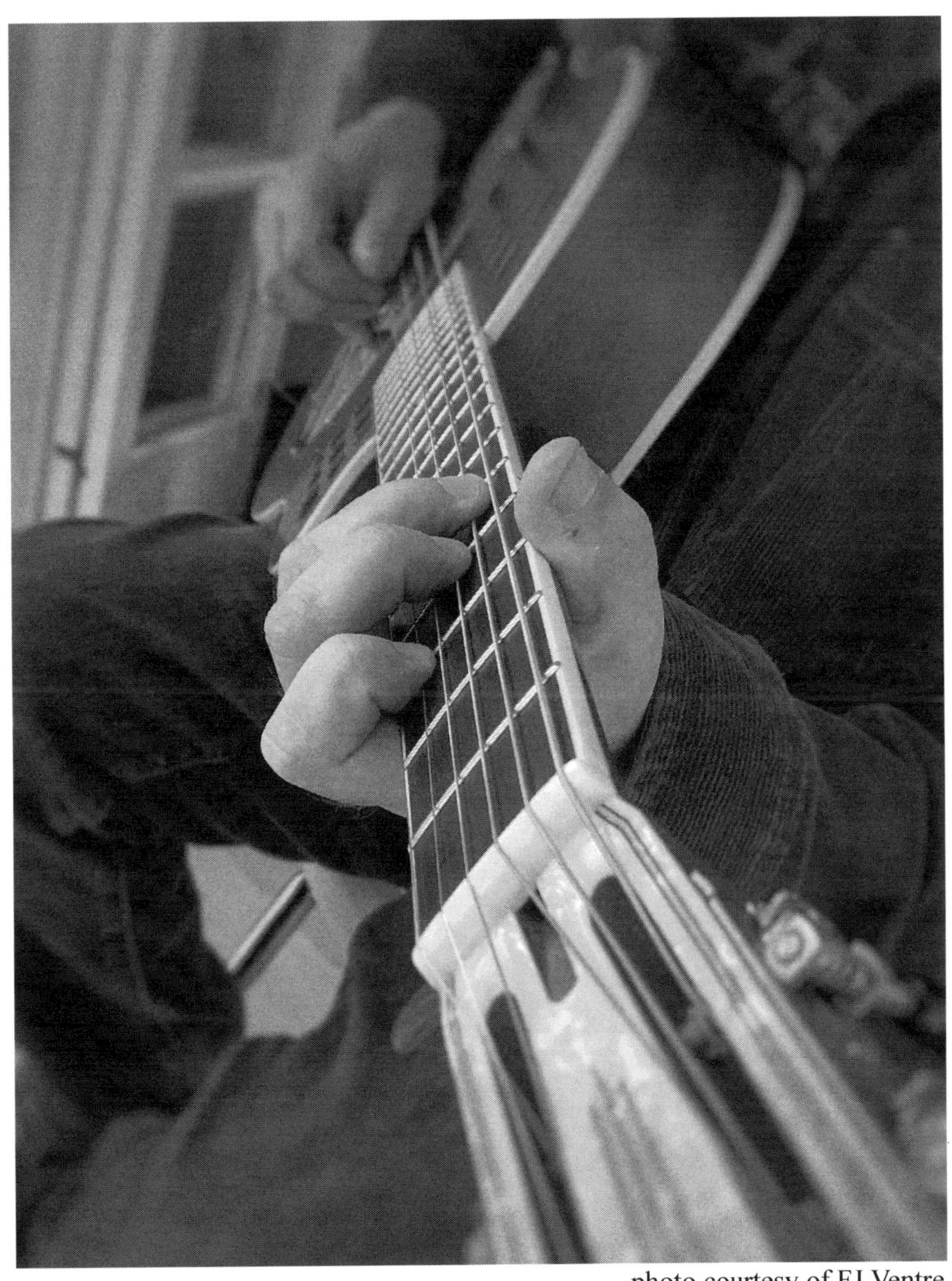

photo courtesy of FJ Ventre

Crazy Blues

Written by Perry Bradford

W. C. Handy tried to interest Black women singers in recording his music but was initially unsuccessful. In 1920, songwriter Perry Bradford persuaded the great Mamie Smith to record several of his non-blues songs, published by Handy, and accompanied by a white band. After that success, Mamie Smith sang his "Crazy Blues", also published by Handy, and it became a hit. Some people regard that 1920 version of "Crazy Blues" as the first time a true blues tune was recorded.

A

I can't sleep at night, I can't eat a bite
'Cause the gal I love she don't treat me right
She makes me feel so blue, I don't know what to do
Sometimes I sit and sigh and then begin to cry
'Cause my best friend said her last goodbye

B

There's a change in the ocean, change in the deep blue sea, my baby
I tell you folks, there ain't no change in me
My love for that gal will always be

C

Now I got the crazy blues since my baby went away
I ain't got no time to lose, I must find her today
Now the doctor's gonna do all that he can
But what you're gonna need is an undertaker man
I ain't had nothing' but bad news - and now I got the crazy blues

B

Now I can read her letters, I sure can't read her mind
I thought she's lovin' me, she's leavin' all the time
Now I see my poor love was blind

I went down to the railroad, stick my head on the track
Thought about my baby, I gladly snatched it back
Now my baby's gone, she gave me the sack

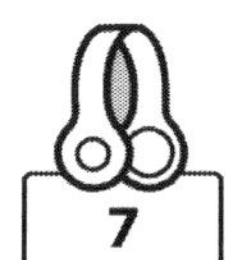

Crazy Blues

by Perry Bradford (arranged for guitar by Jon Shain)

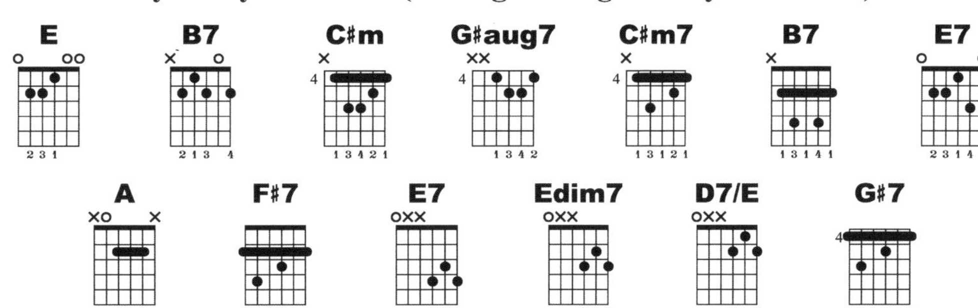

Standard tuning

♩ = 104

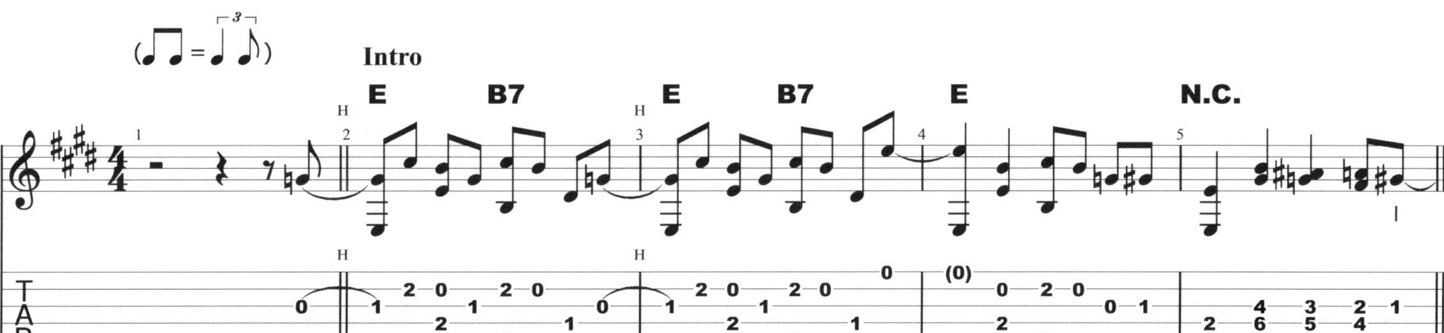

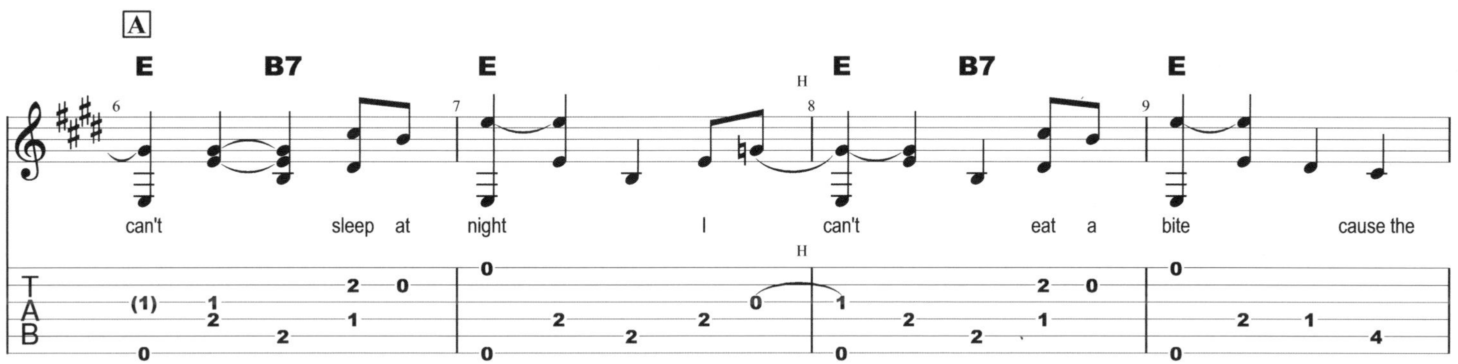

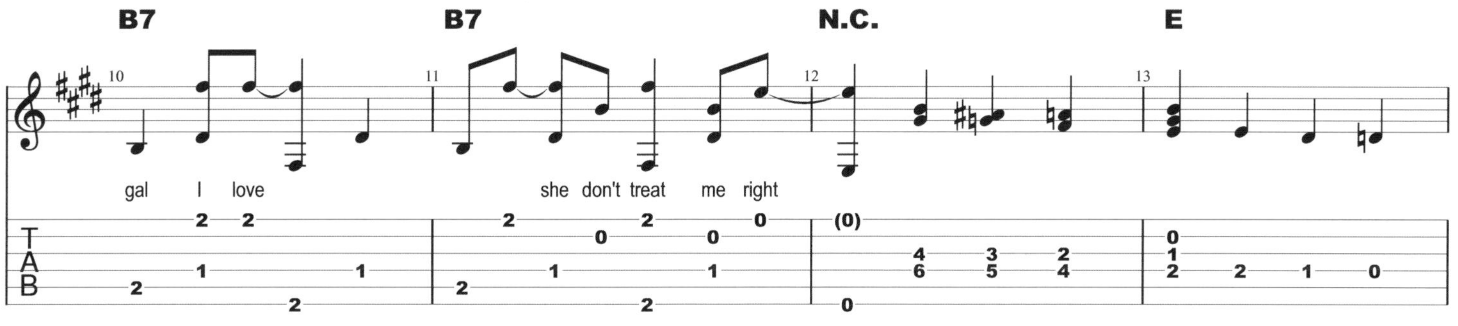

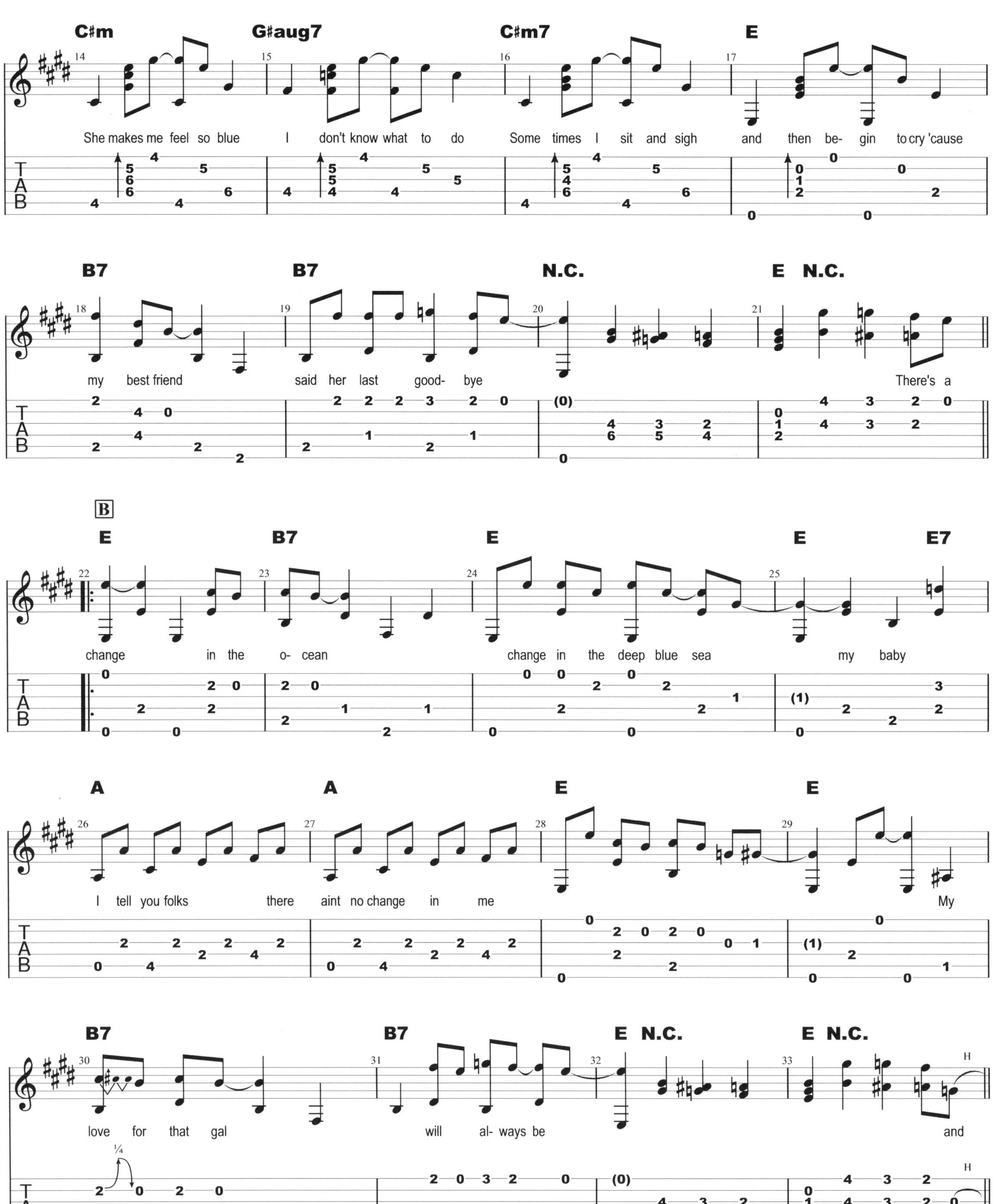
C♯m G♯aug7 C♯m7 E
She makes me feel so blue I don't know what to do Some times I sit and sigh and then be- gin to cry 'cause
B7 B7 N.C. E N.C.
my best friend said her last good- bye There's a
B
E B7 E E E7
change in the o- cean change in the deep blue sea my baby
A A E E
I tell you folks there aint no change in me My
B7 B7 E N.C. E N.C.
love for that gal will al- ways be and
¼
H
T
A
B

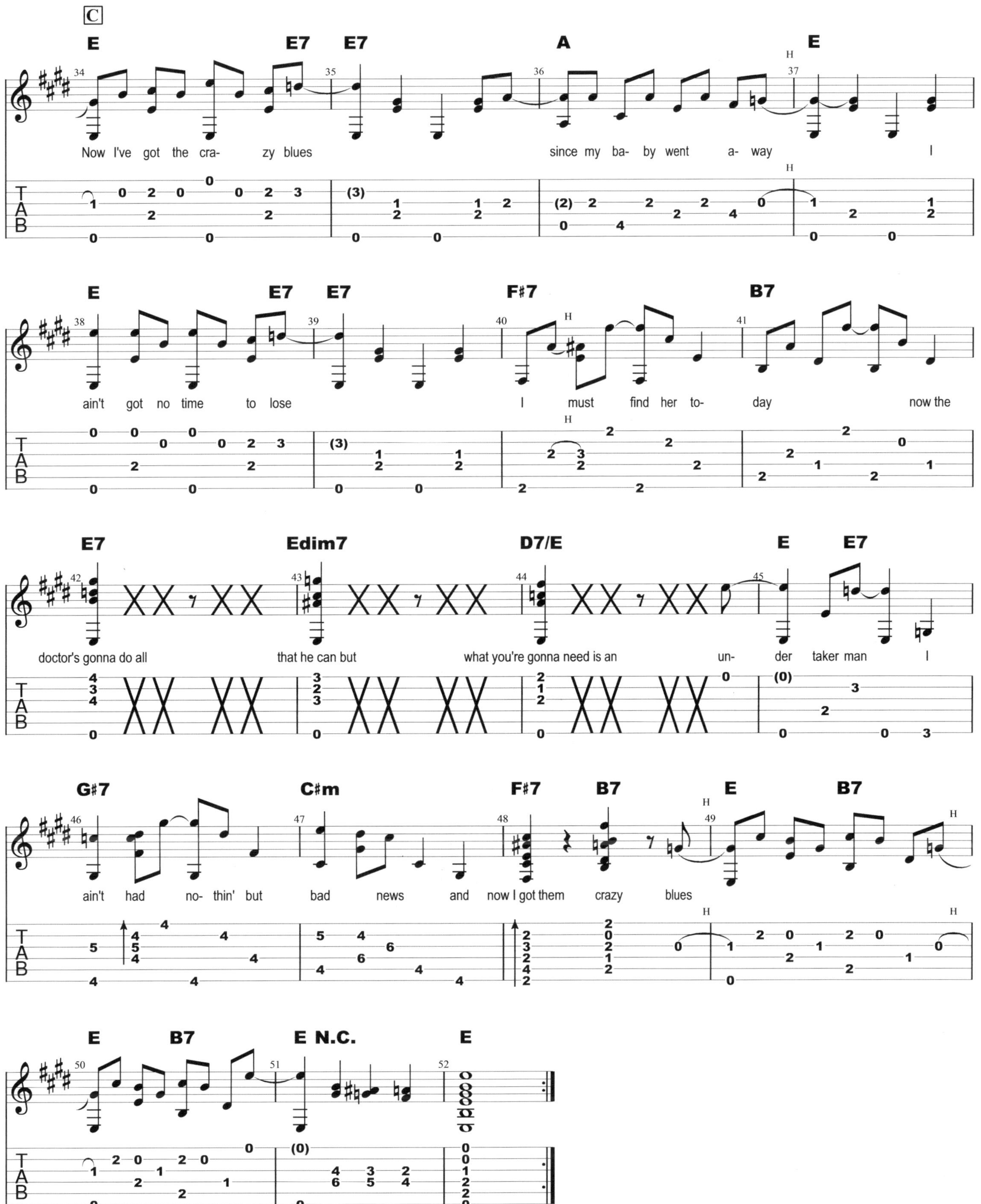
C
E E7 E7 A E
Now I've got the cra- zy blues since my ba- by went a- way I
E E7 E7 F♯7 B7
ain't got no time to lose I must find her to- day now the
E7 Edim7 D7/E E E7
doctor's gonna do all that he can but what you're gonna need is an un- der taker man I
G♯7 C♯m F♯7 B7 E B7
ain't had no- thin' but bad news and now I got them crazy blues
E B7 E N.C. E

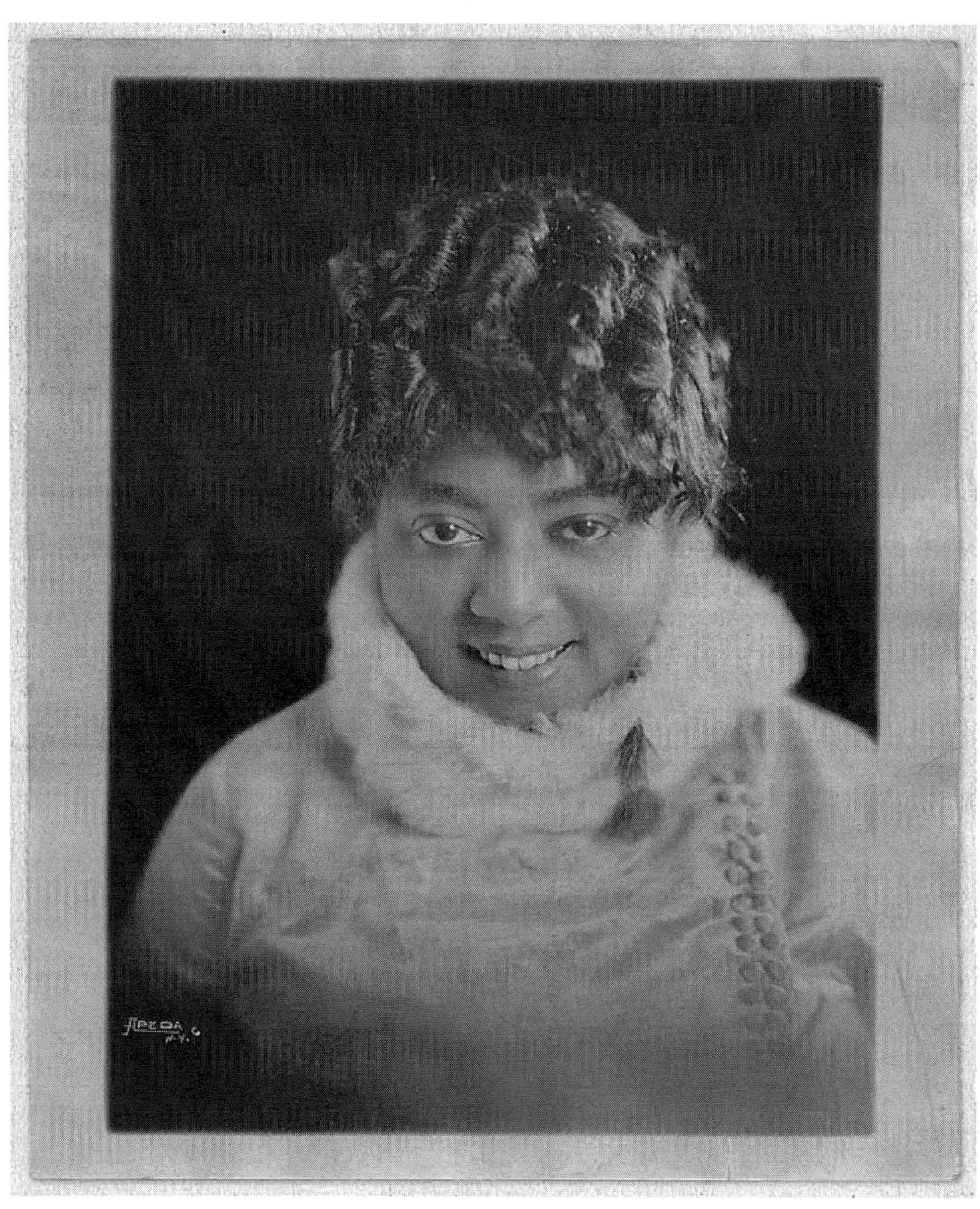

Mamie Smith

That Thing Called Love

Written by Perry Bradford

This song is one of the "non-blues" tunes that Perry Bradford wrote and Mamie Smith sang in 1920 before recording "Crazy Blues". It may not be a classic "blues" chord progression or melody in the strictest sense, but the heartbroken sentiment fits in alongside a set of blues material and Mamie Smith's version was a big hit in that early period of recording and a historic ground-breaker. "That Thing Called Love" was the first recording by a Black woman.

A

I'm worried in my mind
I'm worried all the time
My babe she called to say
That she was going away to stay

Now I love her deep down in my heart
But the best of friends must part
Now I want somebody, please
To cure me of my love disease

B

That thing called love will make you sick inside
That thing called love that money can not buy
Make you sad, Make you glad
Will even drive your mama mad

That thing called love has such a funny feelin'
Thing called love will set your brain a-reelin'
When you're alone and feelin' blue
You think 'bout someone who don't care for you
There's nobody knows what that thing called love will do

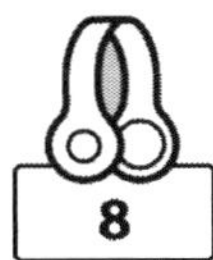

That Thing Called Love

by Perry Bradford (arranged for guitar by Jon Shain)

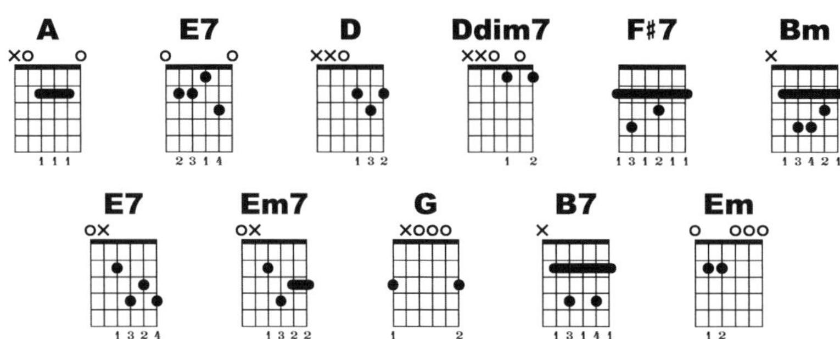

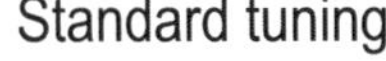

♩ = 111

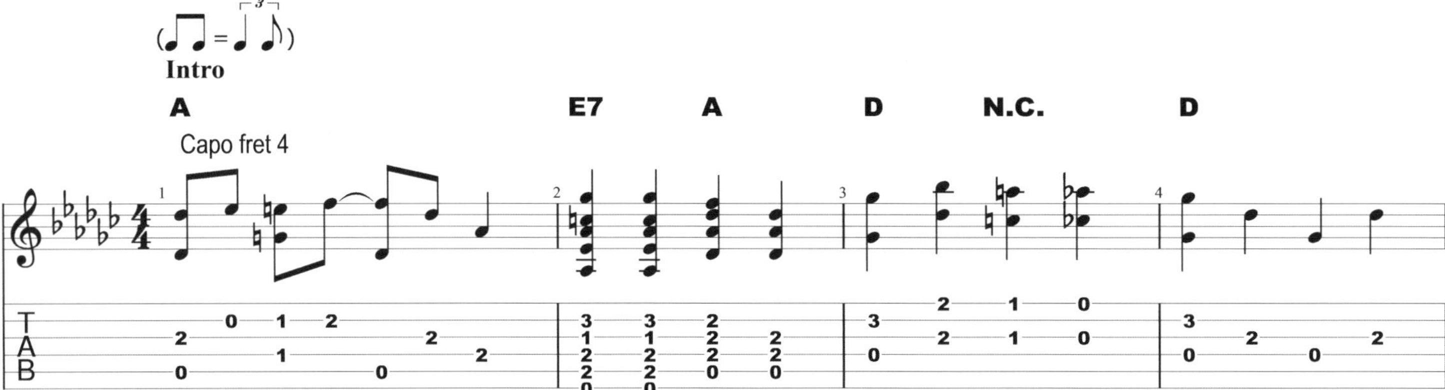

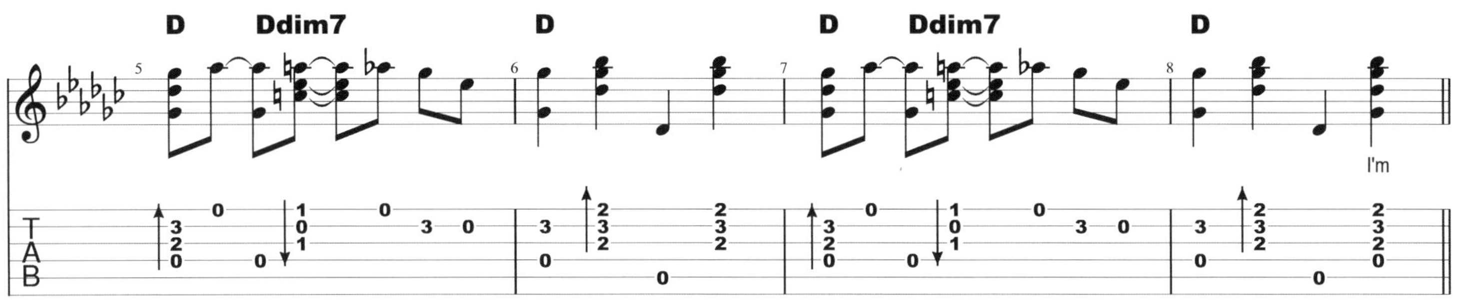

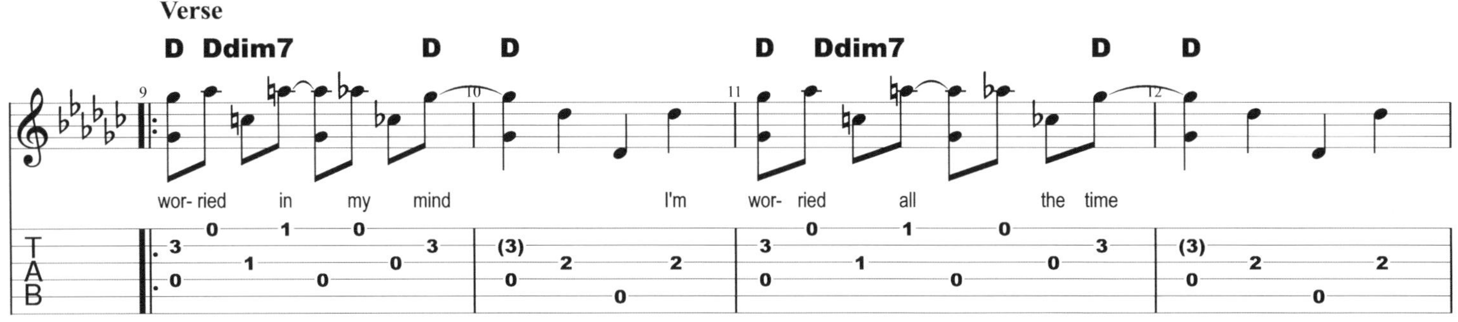

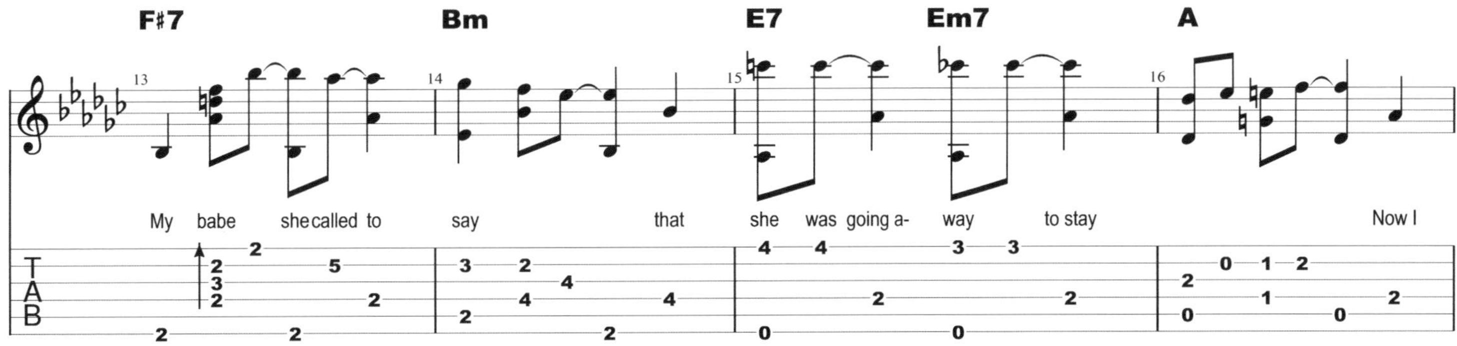
F♯7 Bm E7 Em7 A
My babe she called to say that she was going a- way to stay Now I

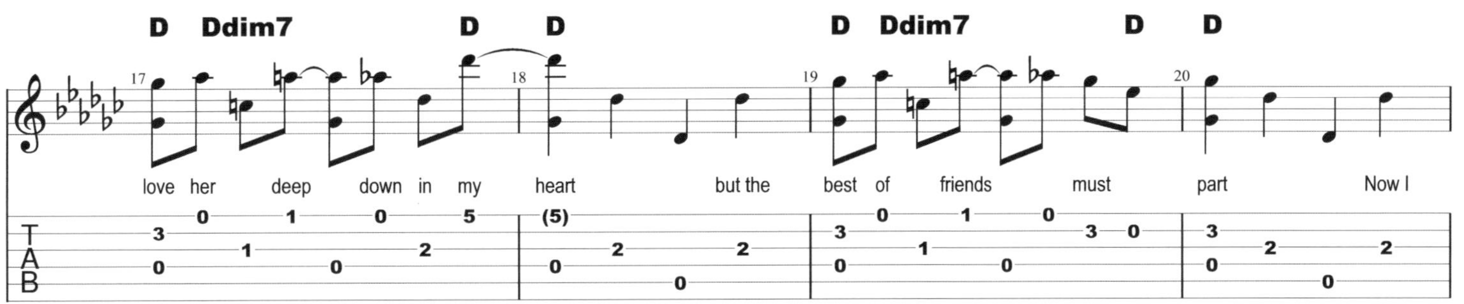
D Ddim7 D D D Ddim7 D D
love her deep down in my heart but the best of friends must part Now I

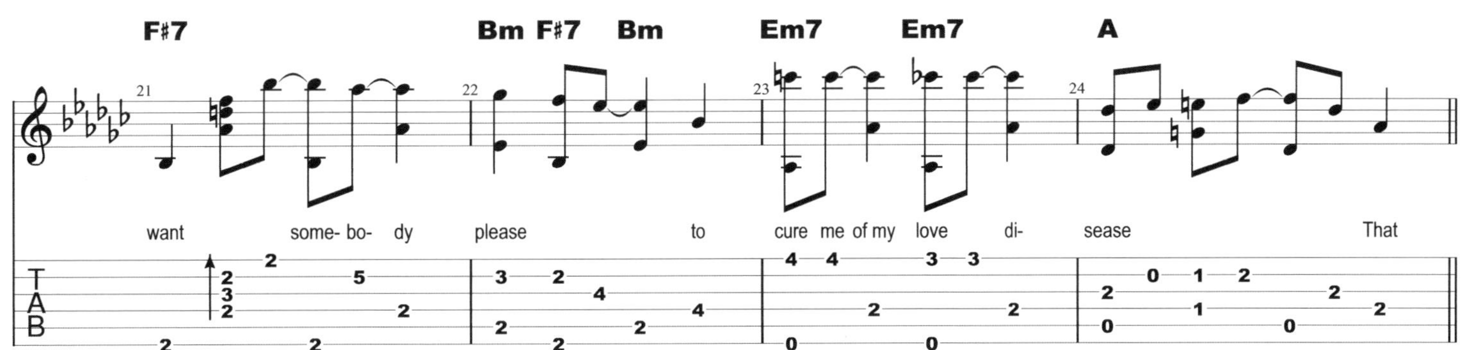
F♯7 Bm F♯7 Bm Em7 Em7 A
want some- bo- dy please to cure me of my love di- sease That

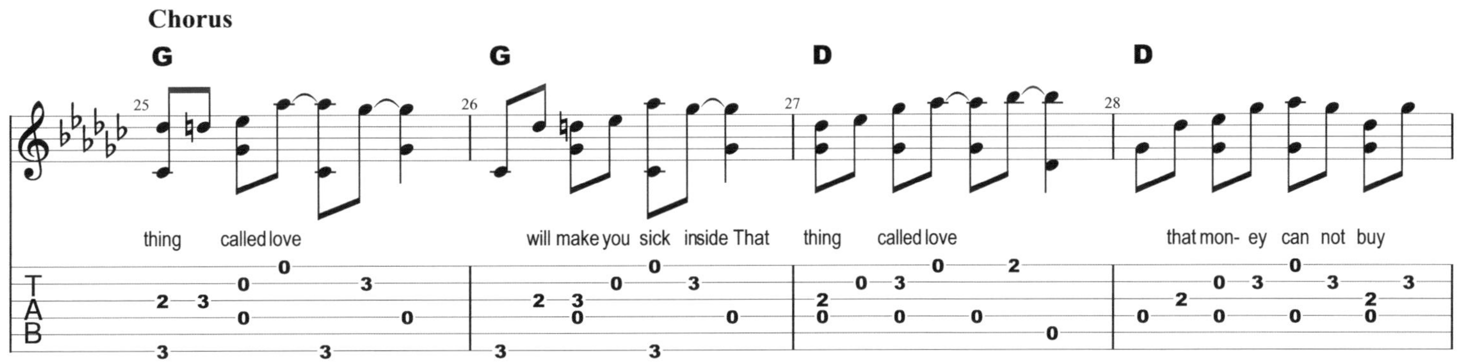
Chorus
G G D D
thing called love will make you sick inside That thing called love that mon- ey can not buy

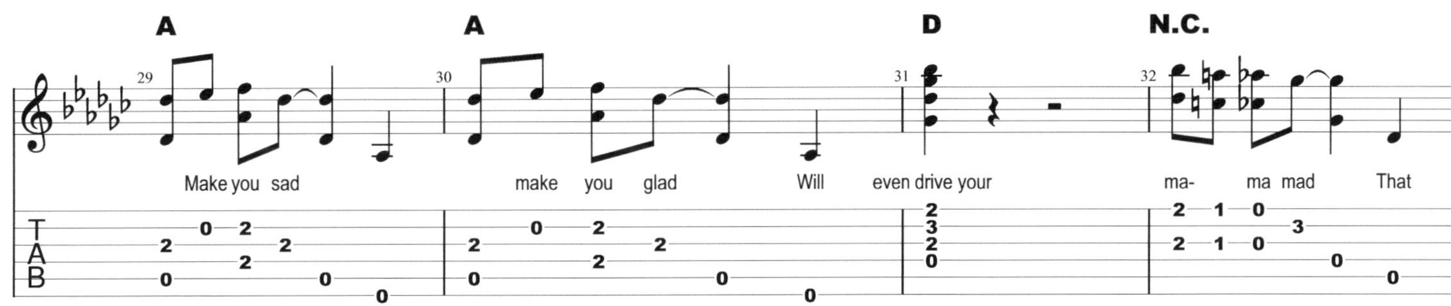
A A D N.C.
Make you sad make you glad Will even drive your ma- ma mad That

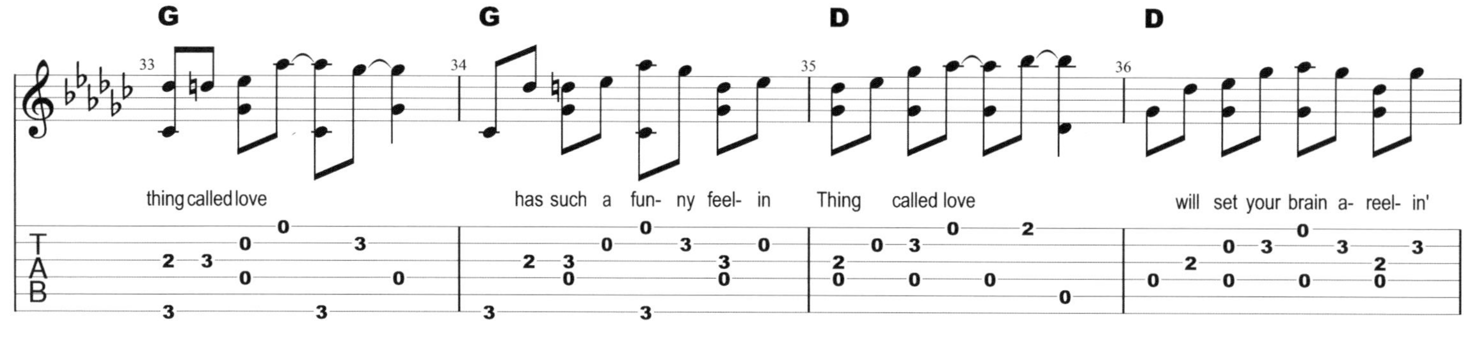
G G D D
thing called love has such a fun- ny feel- in Thing called love will set your brain a- reel- in'

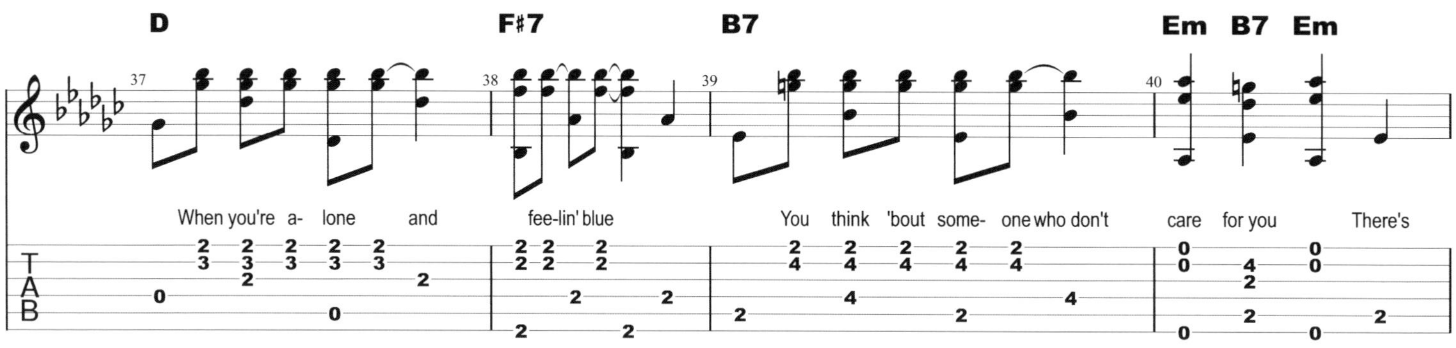
D F♯7 B7 Em B7 Em
When you're a- lone and fee-lin' blue You think 'bout some- one who don't care for you There's

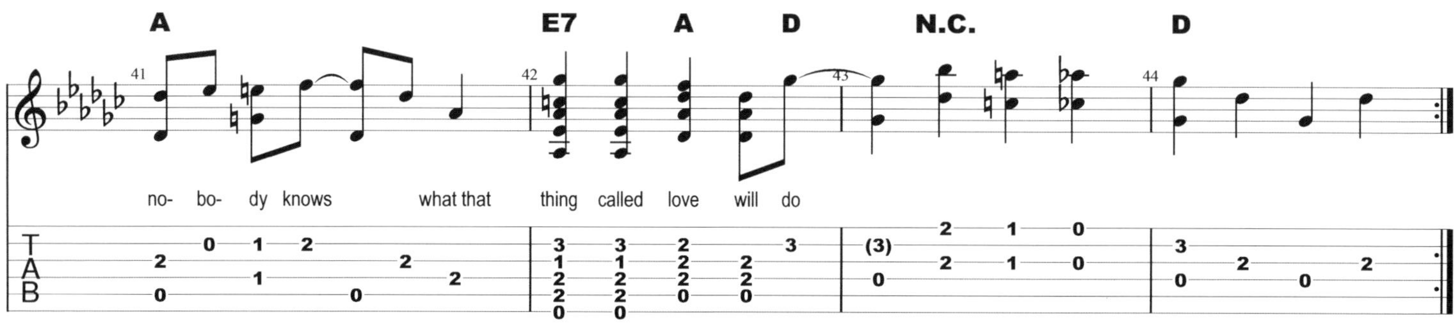
A E7 A D N.C. D
no- bo- dy knows what that thing called love will do

Outro

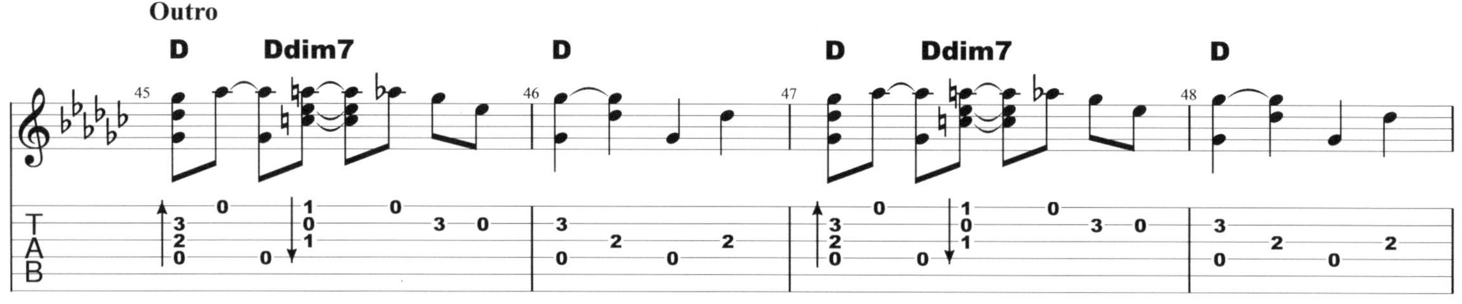
D Ddim7 D D Ddim7 D

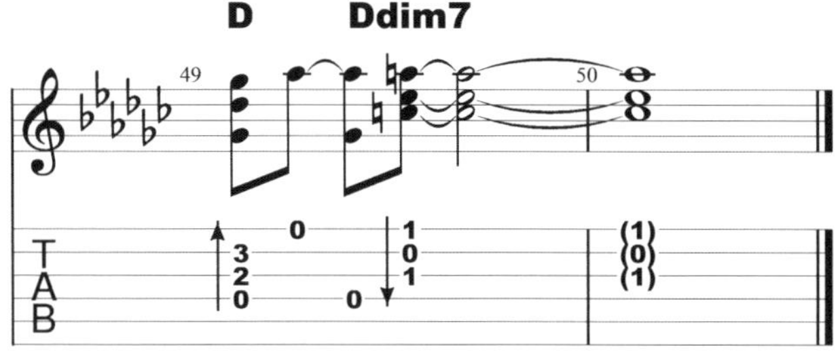
D Ddim7

Deep River Blues

Written by Eddie Green and Lucile Marie Handy

"Deep River Blues" dates to 1924 (the baby of this collection of songs) and was written by Eddie Green with music by Lucile Marie Handy, the daughter of W. C. Handy. Two women, Rosa Henderson and Lucile's sister Katherine Handy, both recorded "Deep River Blues" in 1924. But the song became a hit when it was recorded by Willard Robinson in 1928. It was an audience favorite of his band which became called the "Deep River Orchestra". This song is not the same "Deep River Blues" associated with Doc Watson.

A

Deep river, deep river, Mississippi River so deep and wide
My heart is breaking as I watch the evening tide
Because I'm over here and my gal is on the other side

Deep river, deep river, when I feel worried I come to you
I come and sit beside you when I'm feeling blue
'Cause you're the only one I can tell my troubles to

B

If I had the means, I'd go to New Orleans
But right at this time I ain't got a dime to spare

At the break of day, you'll find me gone away
There's no one to care or want to know where I'm gone

If I get the blues then I will take off my shoes
I'll look to the Lord and jump overboard and drown

C

Deep river blues, I can't refuse
Your sweet melody, I'll always be
By your side when the evening tide comes along

Deep River Blues

by Eddie Green and Lucile Marie Handy
(arranged for guitar by Jon Shain)

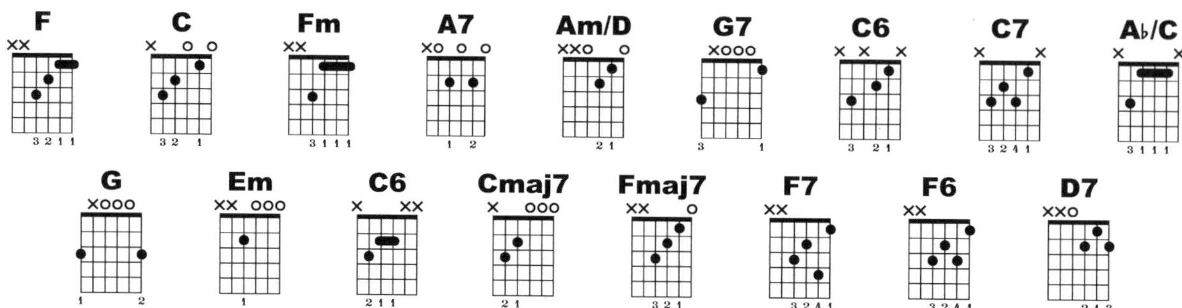

Standard tuning

♩ = 105

Intro

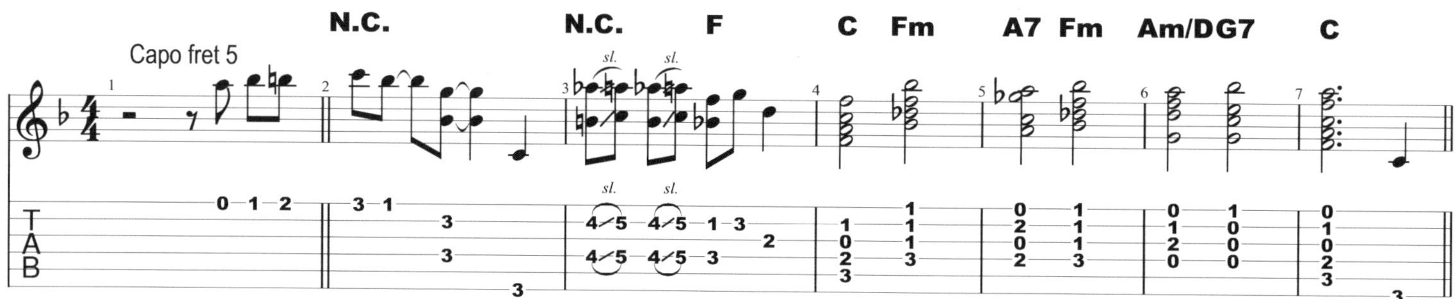

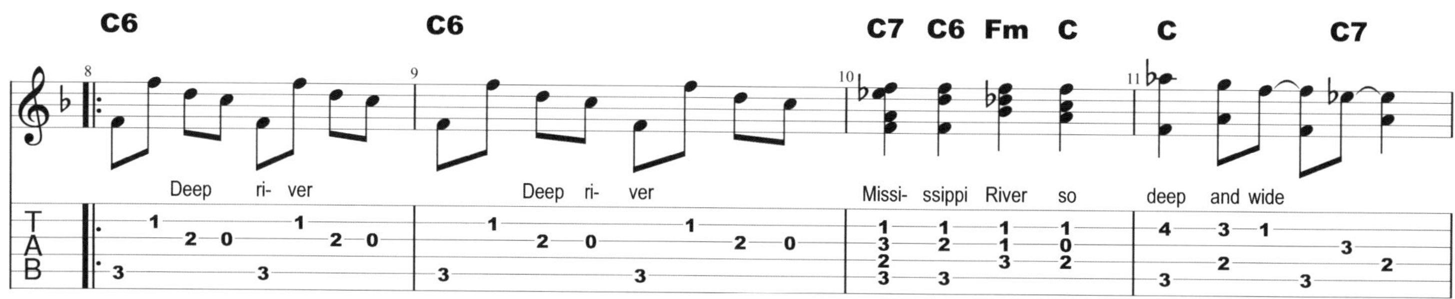

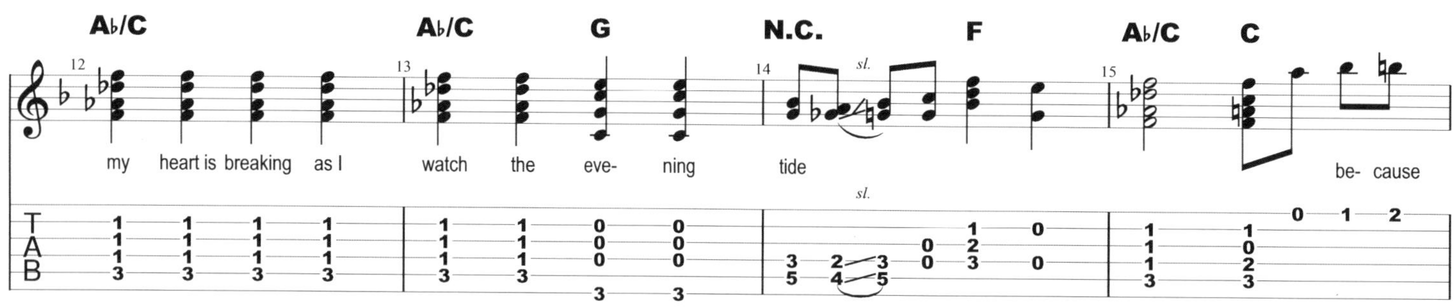

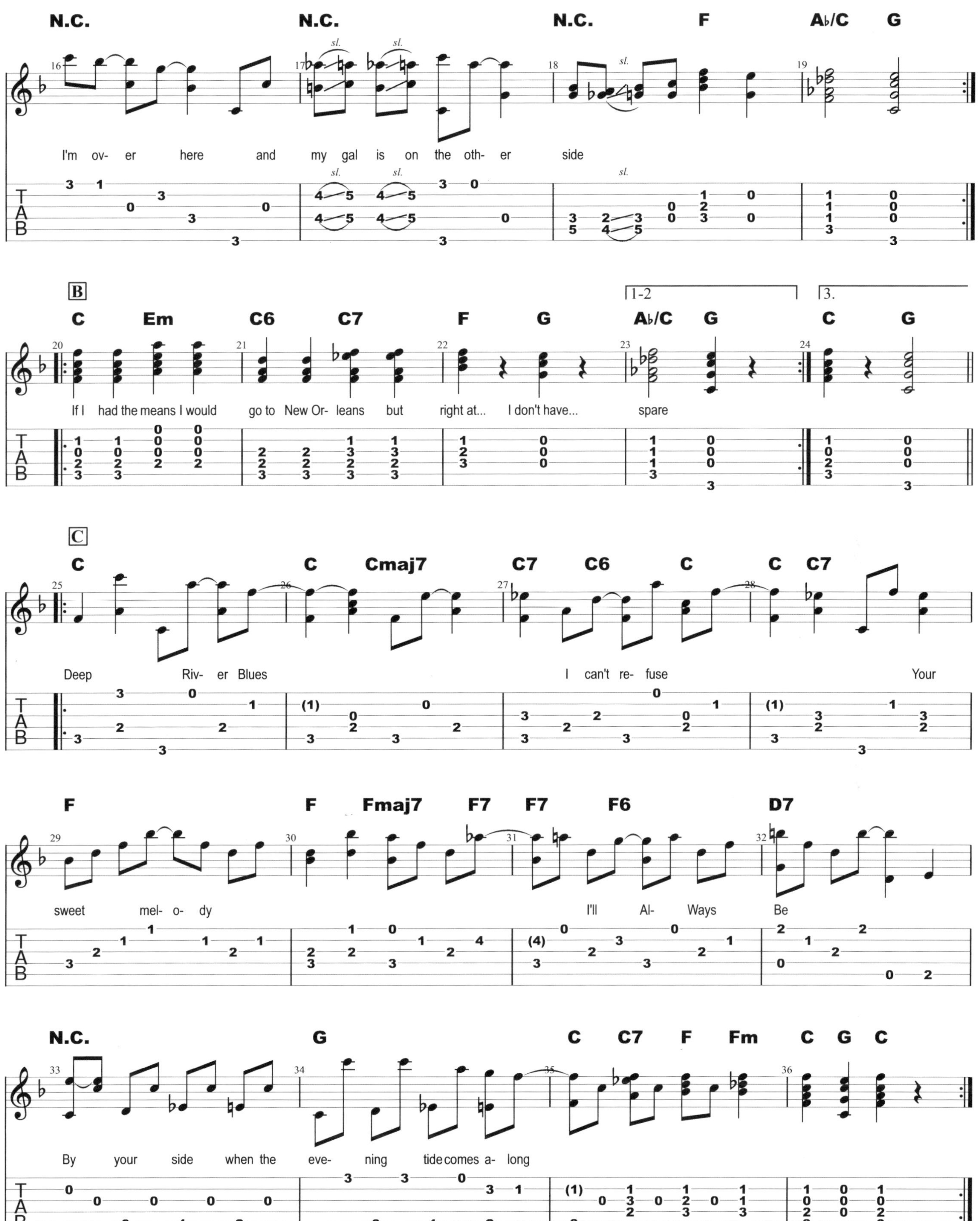
N.C. N.C. N.C. F A♭/C G
I'm ov- er here and my gal is on the oth- er side
sl.
B
1-2
3.
C Em C6 C7 F G A♭/C G C G
If I had the means I would go to New Or- leans but right at... I don't have... spare
C
C C Cmaj7 C7 C6 C C C7
Deep Riv- er Blues I can't re- fuse Your
F F Fmaj7 F7 F7 F6 D7
sweet mel- o- dy I'll Al- Ways Be
N.C. G C C7 F Fm C G C
By your side when the eve- ning tide comes a- long
TAB

Down Home Blues
Written by Tom Delaney

Tom Delaney was one of the more popular and prolific composers of blues songs in the 1920's. Much of his material was fodder for the recording artists and publishers of the era, since they were always on the lookout for new blues following the huge success of Perry Bradford and Mamie's Smith's "Crazy Blues". Delaney's "Down Home Blues", recorded in 1923 and released in 1924, was a fantastic success for the great Ethel Waters. I changed some of the words back to the original lyrics from her recorded version. She sang, "He broke my heart… how I'd love to break his face". Somehow, I don't think I'd get away with that sentiment in today's day!

A

I never felt so lonesome before
My baby quit me this time, she's gone for sure
And she's broke my heart for I loved her true
So now I'm worried, lonesome, and blue

B

And I've got the blues on my mind
I just feel like crying all the time

C

Woke up this morning, the day was dawning
My lovin' baby was not about
She got that lovin' that always makes me shout
And I hope she comes back before it all gives out

Now she was no true gal, but then a new gal
Could ever tempt me or make me glad
Yes I need a good gal, I need a good gal bad
Just 'cause I ain't been gotten that don't mean I can't be had

Some gals like me 'cause I'm happy, some 'cause I dress snappy
Some call me honey, quite a few think I've got money
Then again some tell me Daddy, you sure smell sweet
So if you put that all together, That makes me everything a good gal needs

So there's no use in grieving, folks, I'm leaving
I'm brokenhearted and Dixie bound
Oh, I've been mistreated, ain't got no time to lose
Yes, my train is waiting, I've got the down home blues

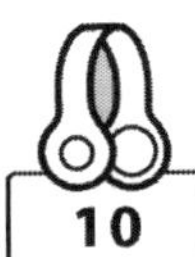

Down Home Blues

by Tom Delaney (arranged for guitar by Jon Shain)

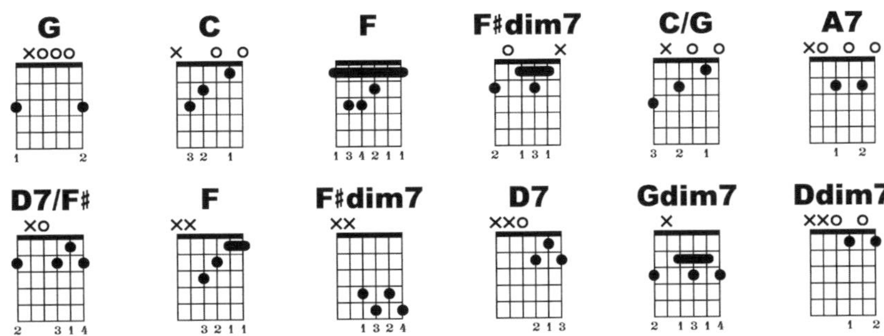

Standard tuning

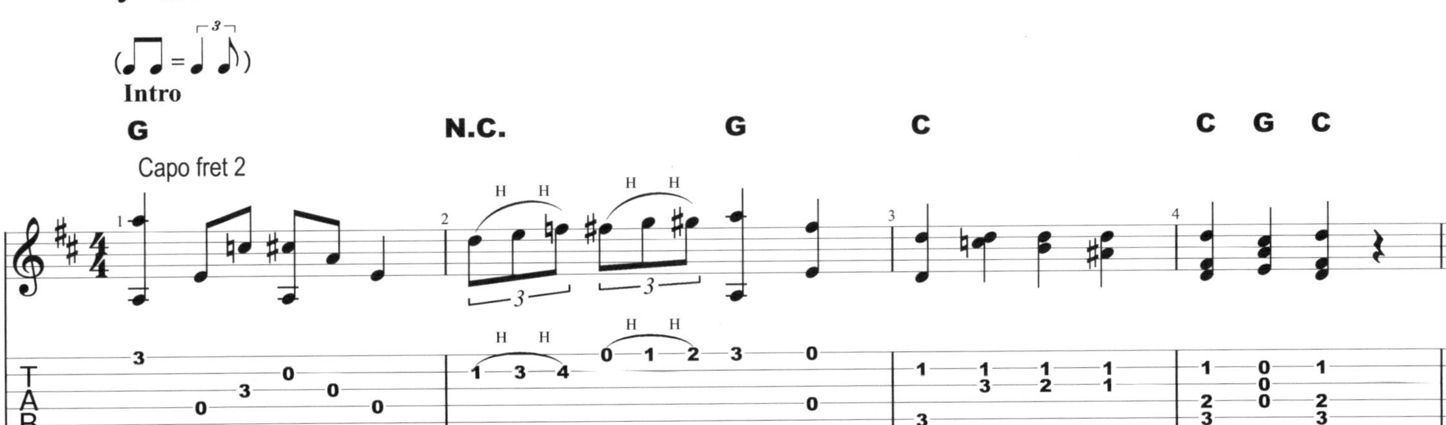

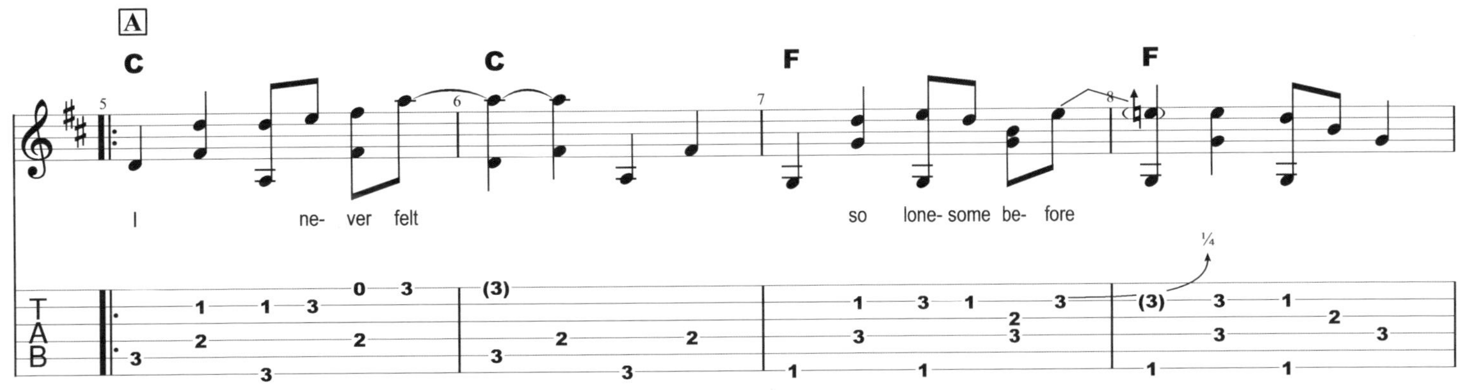

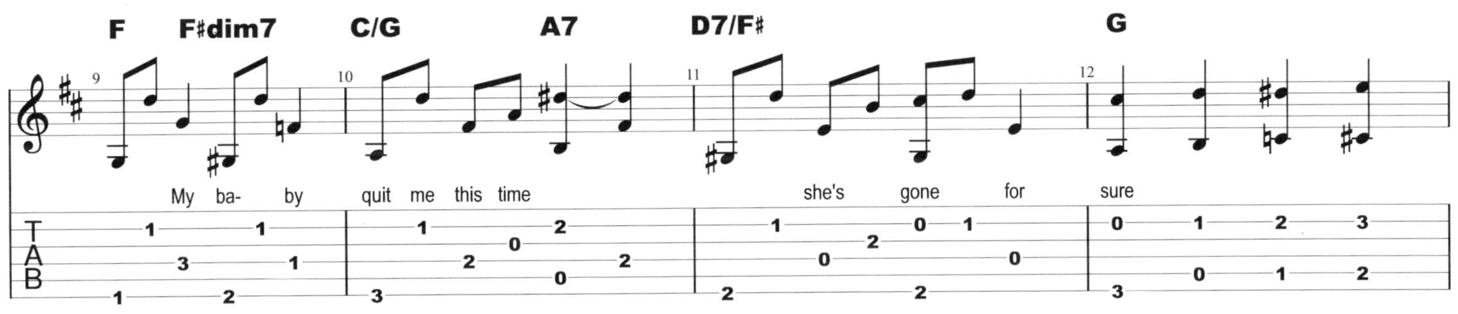

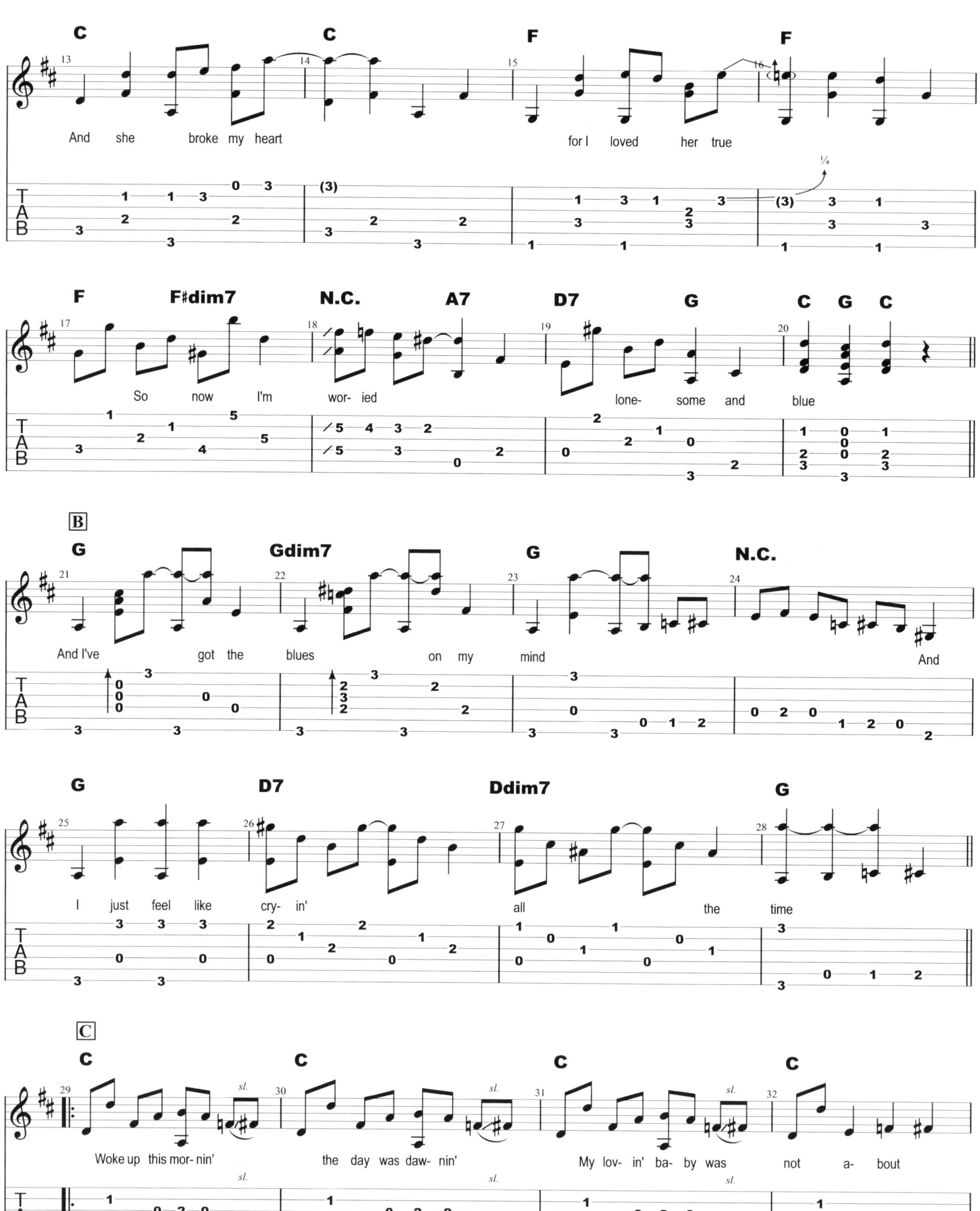
C
C
F
F
And she broke my heart
for I loved her true
F
F♯dim7
N.C.
A7
D7
G
C G C
So now I'm wor- ied
lone- some and blue
B
G
Gdim7
G
N.C.
And I've got the blues on my mind
And
G
D7
Ddim7
G
I just feel like cry- in'
all the time
C
C
C
C
C
Woke up this mor- nin'
the day was daw- nin'
My lov- in' ba- by was not a- bout

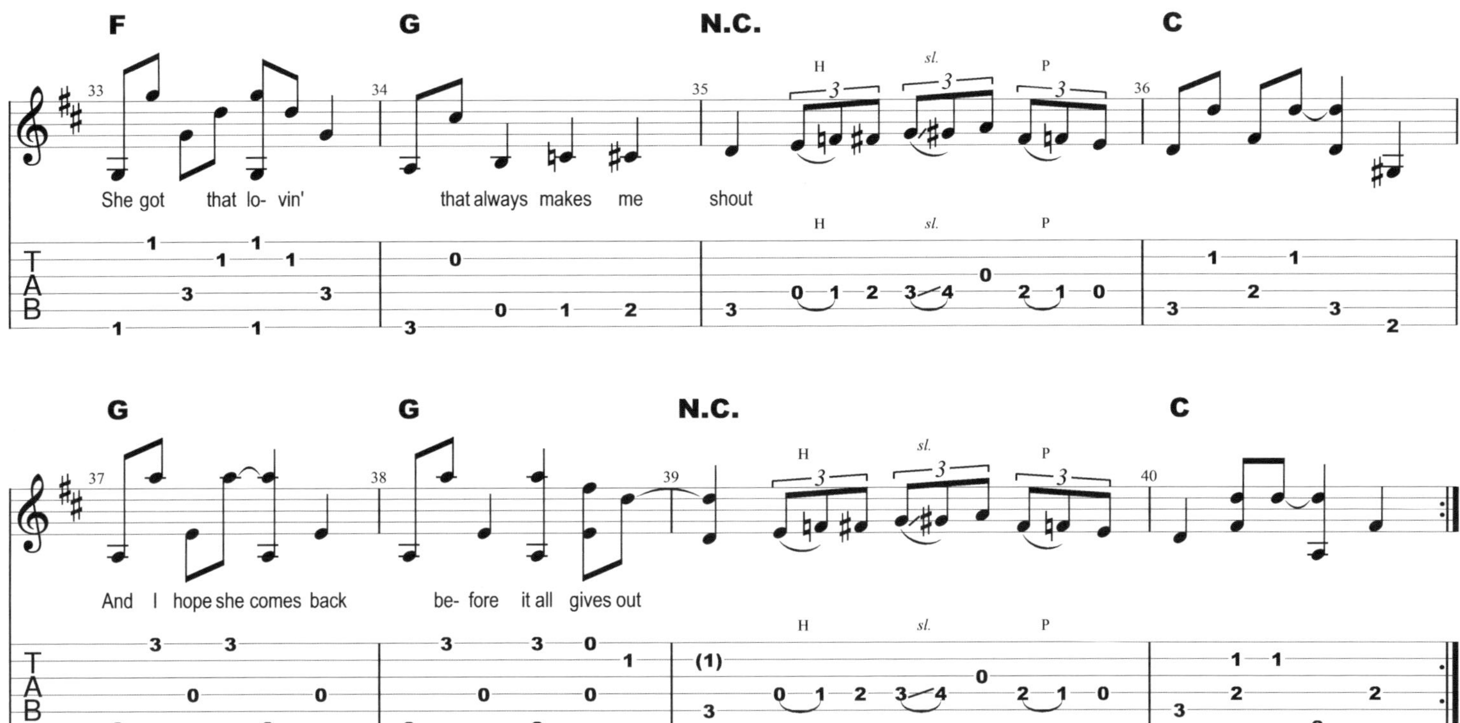
F
G
N.C.
C
She got that lo- vin' that always makes me shout
H
sl.
P
G
G
N.C.
C
And I hope she comes back be- fore it all gives out
H
sl.
P

About the Author

Jon Shain is a veteran singer-songwriter who's been turning heads for years with his words, his fiery acoustic guitar work, and his evolved musical style – combining improvised piedmont blues with bluegrass, swing, and ragtime. He is the 2019 winner of the International Blues Challenge in the solo/duo category. Shain's award-winning disc, *Gettin' Handy with the Blues: A Tribute to the Legacy of W. C. Handy*, was released in January 2018. Shain's most recent duo album with long-time collaborator FJ Ventre, *Never Found a Way to Tame the Blues*, was released in 2021.

Jon grew up in Haverhill, Massachusetts, a Merrimack River mill-town that had already seen its better days by the time he was a child in the 1970s. His family's business was a small textile dyeing company, and he worked in the factory during the summers throughout his teens. At the same time, Shain began to discover his love of American roots music and songwriting, specifically drawn to the narratives about regular people and themes of social justice.

Shain headed south to North Carolina in 1986, to study American History at Duke University and to continue his musical journey, as well. In addition to studying with jazz professor Paul Jeffrey, he also had the good fortune to learn the piedmont blues tradition firsthand by playing in Big Boy Henry's backing band. It was at this time that Shain also got to meet and play with John Dee Holeman and a number of the great older NC blues players. Shain's classes in school were heavily concentrated in southern history, English, and world religions. That mixture of the academic environment and the real-world blues music is what has most informed his musical direction.

Shain cut his touring teeth from 1989-1998 founding the Chapel Hill, NC folk-rock group, Flyin' Mice and their spin-off group, WAKE. The band performed with acts such as David Grisman, Tony Rice Unit, Hot Tuna, and the Dixie Dregs, released four CDs, and played clubs, schools, and festivals up and down the East Coast, building a legion of fans.

After his band's breakup, Shain went solo, returning to his roots in the folk and blues circuit. In addition to two albums with FJ Ventre and one with Joe Newberry, Jon has released ten albums of his own folk-blues compositions. Shain and Ventre also recently produced Donna Herula's blues radio chart-topping album, *Bang at the Door*.

The last several years has seen Shain and Ventre headlining listening rooms on the East Coast, in the Midwest, and in Europe, as well as opening shows for John Hiatt, Keb' Mo', Little Feat, and others. When Shain is not recording, producing other artists, or performing, he stays busy giving private instruction in Piedmont blues fingerstyle guitar, and teaching group workshops in songwriting and blues guitar.

For more information or to contact Jon, please go to www.jonshain.com